MAURICE BERESFORD

WALKS ROUND RED BRICK

A NEW EDITION

additional text by

Christopher Hammond

with photographs by

Ruth Baumberg

The Thoresby Society
The Leeds Philosophical and Literary Society

2012

ISSN 0082 – 4232
ISBN 978 0 900741 71 5

To the memory of Lulu
companion in these walks during 1977 and 1978
whose four feet were usually there first

Front cover illustration – The Gateway to Clothworkers' Court
Back cover illustration – The Arms of the Clothworkers' Company
sculpted in the façade of The School of Design.

CONTENTS

FOREWORD

MELVYN BRAGG
CHANCELLOR OF THE UNIVERSITY OF LEEDS

ARCHITECTURE HAS ALWAYS been a potent symbol of wealth, status and power; serving to express the animating ideal of the times.

The English civic university movement of the nineteenth and early twentieth centuries created institutions which admitted men without reference to religion or social background and emphasised the importance of practical skills as well as academic theory. The democratic ideals and the strength of ambition of the pioneers who came together to create these institutions is clearly reflected in the solidity and confidence of the original red brick architecture, such as Alfred Waterhouse's Great Hall at Leeds – these were institutions built to last. As the University of Leeds developed, so its campus grew and its architectural style evolved to reflect the changing times – in Portland stone, such as the iconic Parkinson Building, and in the ferro-concrete of the buildings that were part of the famous Chamberlin plan, which are still provoking lively debate today, as they did when they were constructed.

One of the things that has changed my life over the past few years is the discovery that city walking can be as intriguing and satisfying as country walking. In this new edition of Maurice Beresford's classic civic walking guide, Christopher Hammond and Ruth Baumberg have borne this out. Not only have they produced a detailed handbook to the richly diverse architecture of the University and its environs that is both diverting and informative; in following Beresford's footsteps, the walks they have mapped out also vividly tell the story of the social history of one of our great Victorian cities and the rise of one of our country's greatest successes – our world class universities.

MAURICE BERESFORD'S BOOK *Walks Round Red Brick*, published by Leeds University Press in 1980, has become a much sought after classic: its easy and readable style is, as in all his other works, founded upon a deep and meticulous scholarship. Moreover as a work of literature it cannot be regarded as 'out of date'.

My objective, in accordance with the wishes of the Leeds Philosophical and Literary Society and Thoresby Society (of which for many years Maurice Beresford held the position of Patron) has been to extend the *Walks* and to include additional material on the University buildings – from its founding as the Yorkshire College of Science in 1874 (the 'of Science' was subsequently dropped), through to its admission as a constituent college of the federal Victoria University (the others being Owens College in Manchester and Liverpool College) and finally from the inauguration of the University of Leeds in 1904 to the present. These notes, together with those which point out the changed functions and appearances of the buildings Beresford describes (except of course those that are now demolished), are clearly distinguished from his original text by the use of Univers typeface. Except for some minor changes, corrections and the deletion of material (particularly in Walks XV and XVI) that would otherwise distract a present day reader, Beresford's text is unchanged.

My only qualification for this task stems from my own participation in the *Walks* in the 1970s and my own, later, guided walks in which I very much followed Beresford's (and Lulu's) footsteps. I hope that, in this New Edition, they can again be appreciated by a new generation of readers – either on the ground or, as Beresford says, 'in front of the fire'.

However, perhaps most immediately evident to a reader is the substitution of the original, rather sombre black and white photographs by colour photographs, taken as far as possible from the same viewpoints by Ruth Baumberg. Her photographs considerably enhance the attractiveness of the book. The original maps and plans have been replaced by a modified University Campus Guide which indicates the routes of the *Walks* more clearly.

Finally, a word about the overall change in appearance of the University campus from the 1980s to the present. The improvement has been gradual but no less dramatic: the cleaning and restoration of the buildings, the clearing away of temporary huts and terrapins and their replacement by fine new buildings, the landscaping and planting of trees and of course the almost total exclusion of motor traffic has ensured that Leeds University campus remains one of the finest in the country.

Christopher Hammond (2012)

THE LIFE AND WORK OF MAURICE
BERESFORD FBA (1920-2005)
PATRON OF THE THORESBY SOCIETY 1982-2005

THE THORESBY SOCIETY and all students of the history of Leeds were indeed fortunate when, in 1948, Maurice Beresford was appointed Lecturer in Economic History at the University. He spent the rest of his academic career at Leeds rising to become the first Professor of Economic History in 1959 and Emeritus Professor upon his retirement in 1985.

Maurice Beresford was born in Sutton Coldfield and graduated with a first class degree at Jesus College, Cambridge. His early research and academic reputation were based in the Midlands, where he, along with W. G. Hoskins, established that most of the numerous earthworks and ridges to be seen in the Midland counties were the remains of deserted medieval villages; in doing so he also developed his characteristic approach of combining the historian's traditional study of documents with the study of maps and walking in, and observation of, the landscape. This culminated in his seminal work *The Lost Villages of England* (1954). Almost immediately upon coming to Leeds he 'discovered' the deserted village of Wharram Percy and began his forty year collaboration in its excavation with the late John Hurst. His interests widened to encompass other aspects of the landscape, culminating in two further seminal works: *History on the Ground* (1957) and *New Towns of the Middle Ages* (1967). This latter work, of course, brought him closer to Leeds as one of those new towns.

It was his inaugural lecture as Professor of Economic History, *Time and Place* (1960), which announced his interest in the development of Leeds and which was the increasing focus of his research for the rest of his life. In the lecture he defined the 'Beresfordian approach' to economic history as:

an emphasis on visual things. By 'visual things' I mean not only the traditional sources of historical inquiry, books and documents – they are visual enough; nor do I merely mean maps, a visual summary of the real world. I add the visible real world itself, or rather those visible remains in it by which past economic activity can be detected. In this sense my profession is time and place... I would call my approach a 'field-approach' or 'archeological approach', were it not that 'field' sounds like the country-side and 'archeological' sounds antique.

He proceeded to illustrate this by exploring the impact of field boundaries on the pattern of streets and houses within yards of the university and demonstrating how a single street – Prosperity Street – illustrated in its different groups of houses the building cycles of the last quarter of the nineteenth century. At the same time he was beginning to explore the property deeds held by the University as it expanded its campus; work that culminated in his *Walks Round Red Brick* (1980), intended originally to 'remind the members of the University that they were surrounded in their daily work by a free open air museum of architectural and social history'.

In his contribution 'Prosperity Street and Others' to *Leeds and its Region* (1967), the canvas is widened to a discussion of how the eighteenth-century town initially accommodated the expansion of population after 1770 in its yards and gardens and how the wealthier inhabitants attempted to establish a more salubrious suburb to the west of the town – only for it to be overwhelmed by industrialisation. Four years later his chapter on 'The Back-to-Back House in Leeds, 1787-1937' in *The History of Working Class Housing* (1971), explored the history of the east end of the town and its characteristic building, demonstrating yet again how the pattern of streets and houses reflected the building plots created by the piecemeal sale of fields.

The published culmination of this research was contained in 'The Face of Leeds, 1780-1914' in *A History of Modern Leeds* (1980), edited by D. Fraser, and in the publication of the Thoresby Society's volumes LX and LXI (1985 and 1986): *East End, West End: The Face of Leeds during Urbanisation, 1684-1842*. The first is an invaluable survey of the building development of the whole of the borough, enlivened by the examination of certain streets and districts and by the detailed analysis of photographs. The second volume must be judged Maurice's greatest contribution to our understanding of the development of Leeds township. It is formidable above all in the detail it contains. It will remain an essential reference source for future students, pointing them to new avenues of inquiry and to new source materials.

Professor Beresford's contribution to the history of Leeds goes well beyond his published work. He supervised many postgraduate students whose work contributed to that history. All received a rigorous tutelage in the creative and imaginative use of historical sources. He was also generous in his encouragement and praise of anyone who made a contribution to our understanding of the history of Leeds, whether it be the amateur producing albums of pictures of Leeds townships and suburbs or the professional writing a research paper. Both were beneficiaries of the scribbled notes from Maurice, alerting them to sources he had spotted in record offices which might help them in their research.

Many members will have their own memories of their encounters with Maurice. One who knew him well was Ernest Kirkby who, in an introduction to Professor Beresford's own *Festschrift*, summed him up affectionately as follows:

> There are so many facets both to his character and his achievements. Above all there is Maurice the stimulating teacher, the gifted lecturer, and highly talented, industrious researcher. Then there is the capable administrator and organiser. Those who know him well recognise him as a man who does not suffer fools gladly and who has a strong aversion to the pompous. But there is also the very perceptive, humane and generous man, understanding of the short-comings of others while acknowledging his own weaknesses which fortunately centre only on a penchant for *cordon bleu* cuisine, chocolate and pastries, and getting hooked too easily on some TV 'soaps'. Then there is Maurice a man of culture, Maurice the lover of maps, travel, walking, and railway timetables. And to some students and colleagues there is simply Maurice, 'the Prof with the Dog'.

JIM MORGAN   KEVIN GRADY
Past President   *Member of Council*
The Thoresby Society   *The Thoresby Society*

IN PREPARING THIS New Edition I wish to acknowledge the support of Ann Alexander and David Thornton, joint Editors of the Thoresby Society's Publications and Peter Hirschmann, Chairman of the Publications Committee of the Leeds Philosophical and Literary Society. The inclusion of much new architectural information has been greatly helped by the publication of Susan Wrathmell's *Leeds: Pevsner Architectural Guide* (2005) and Peter Leach's *Yorkshire West Riding: Leeds, Bradford and the North* (2009) in the Pevsner Buildings of England Series. Freda Matthews helped to unravel the estate development complexity in the area of Clarendon Road and Little Woodhouse (Walks XIV-XVI) and I made much use of her *A Walk Round Little Woodhouse* (1997) and *Woodhouse Square* (2005). Kevin Grady (Director of Leeds Civic Trust) and Jim Morgan (formerly President of the Thoresby Society) both former students of Beresford, provided the substance of the biographical note on their former supervisor. Ruth Baumberg's superb photographs are the fruit of very many 'site-visits' particularly in the early mornings to beat the ubiquitous motor car. I am also grateful to English Heritage for permission to reproduce the 1982 photograph of Springfield House.

Finally, I wish to thank Claire McConnell for word processing the entire book and to acknowledge, in particular, her skill in deciphering my handwriting.

KEY

Routes and end limits of the walks

North - South Campus Access Route External

North - South Campus Access Route Internal (may involve lifts)

Parking for Blue Badge or University Disabled Permit holders. There are no cross-campus car routes; please contact the Parking Office on 0113 343 5491 or carparking@leeds.ac.uk for advice.

Accessible entrance serving more than one building

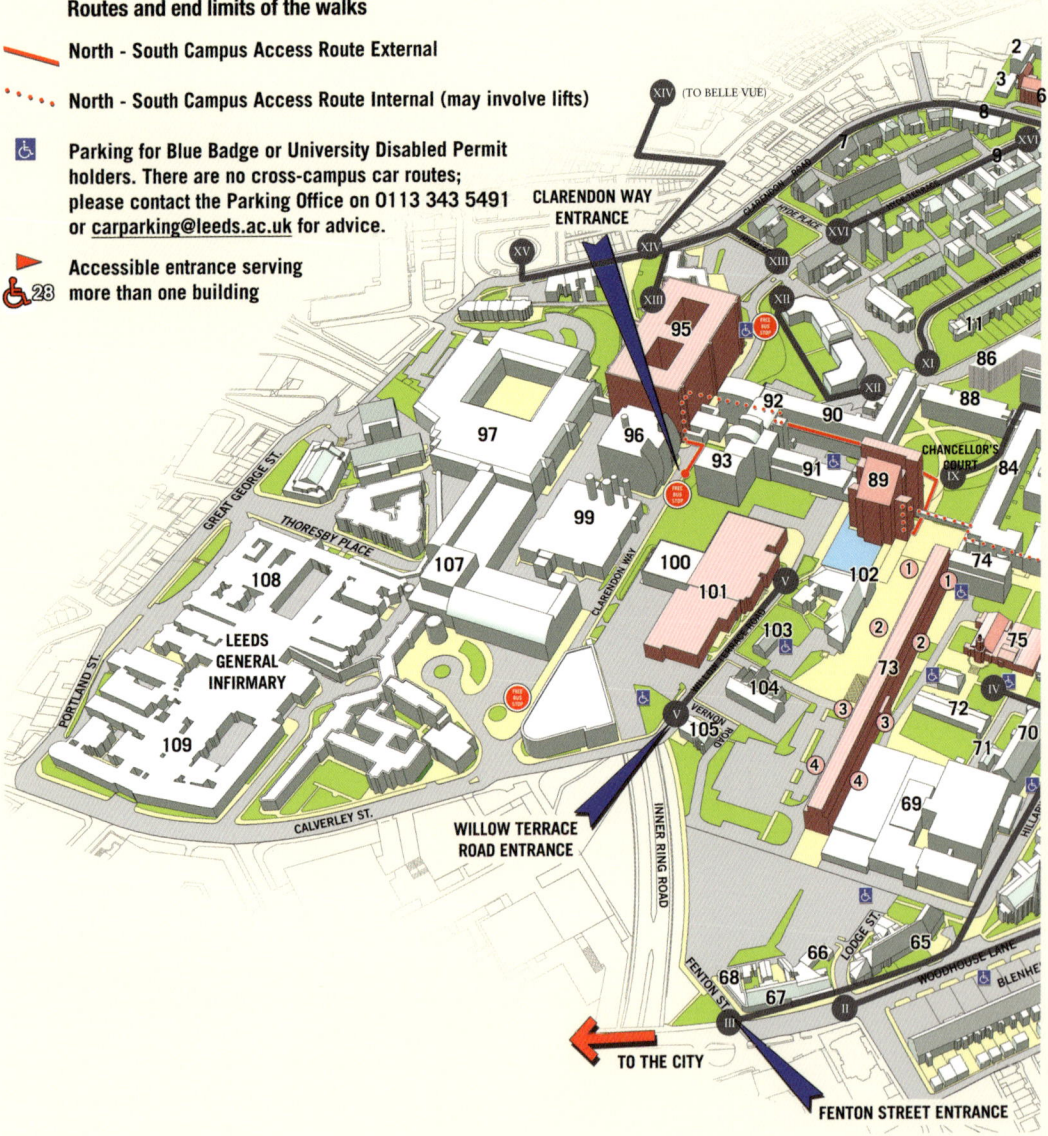

XIV (TO BELLE VUE)

CLARENDON WAY ENTRANCE

XV

XIV

XIII

95

97

96

93

92

90

91

89

CHANCELLOR'S COURT

84

99

100

101

102

74

107

108

LEEDS GENERAL INFIRMARY

109

105

104

103

V

V

73

75

72

71

70

69

66

65

68

67

WILLOW TERRACE ROAD ENTRANCE

TO THE CITY

FENTON STREET ENTRANCE

GREAT GEORGE ST.

THORESBY PLACE

PORTLAND ST.

CALVERLEY ST.

CLARENDON WAY

VERNON RD

INNER RING ROAD

FENTON ST.

LODGE ST.

WOODHOUSE LANE

BLENHE

HILL

2
3
8
6
9
7
11
86
88
16

A key to the buildings encountered in the walks are listed on page xvi

MOUNT PRESTON
STREET
ENTRANCE

WESTERN CAMPUS
ENTRANCE

WESTERN
CAMPUS

UNIVERSITY ROAD
ENTRANCE

CEMETERY ROAD
ENTRANCE

N

ST GEORGE'S
FIELDS

TO
HEADINGLEY

UNIVERSITY
SQUARE

VISITOR
PARKING

MAIN ENTRANCE
VISITOR CAR PARK

WOODHOUSE LANE

BLENHEIM WALK

59/60

Numbers refer to the campus map on pages xiv and xv

IN 1943 A Professor of Spanish at the University of Liverpool writing under the name 'Bruce Truscott' sought a phrase which would contrast the civic universities of the late nineteenth century with the medieval foundations at Oxford and Cambridge. He entitled his book *Red Brick University*, taking as a symbol the favourite building materials of Birmingham, Bristol, Leeds, Liverpool, Manchester, and Sheffield. Since then his terms 'Oxbridge' and 'Redbrick' have become part of the English language, although it must be observed that the first architect employed for academic buildings at Leeds, Alfred Waterhouse, had already designed in red brick for clients at Oxford and Cambridge colleges, and would have preferred terracotta here if the Yorkshire College had been able to afford it.

The architectural style at Leeds remained loyal to red brick until after 1930 when Portland stone and then ferro-concrete replaced it, although none of our Waterhouse red brick had been demolished and there is a great deal of red brick in the backside of the Parkinson Building, the Brotherton Library, the University Union and other smaller creations of the nineteen-thirties.

The red brick academic buildings of Waterhouse and his successors have been treated systematically elsewhere.* The red bricks in the title of the present book are different, since Leeds is now a red brick University in a sense beyond that intended by Truscott. For not only are its own earliest buildings of red brick but they are also set in a context of even older red brick houses, totalling about a

---

* The red brick, Portland stone, ferro-concrete and later University
buildings are now included as part of the *WALKS*. – C. H.

thousand in 1877: these mansions, villas and terraces made up the residential suburb of Woodhouse.

In 1877 Alfred Waterhouse designed the first academic building, the Textiles Department, to fit into the western part of the garden of one of these mansions, Beech Grove, which was not demolished until room was needed for the Dyeing Department in 1884. Some of the smaller villas and many of the terraces were eventually demolished for the extension of the University, particularly between 1955 and 1964, and if the 'Go' quotient of the 'Stop-Go' of public financial policy had been larger the fulfilment of the Chamberlin plan would have replaced virtually all the suburban streets by ferro-concrete. In the event, penury has proved to be the preservationists' best friend, and these *Walks*, which first appeared in the University's house magazine in 1977 and 1978, were designed to remind the members of the University that they were surrounded in their daily work by a free open-air museum of architectural and social history. Indeed, since the University's need for accommodation has always outrun the funds available for new building even in the most affluent days, there are many members of the University working and living in converted house property within these red brick streets.

The *Walks* sprang from a suggestion by Mr Simeon Underwood, and they drew on research work in progress since 1961 for a complete street-by-street building history of central Leeds and Woodhouse. Some of the themes of this larger project inevitably show themselves from time to time in the *Walks*. Their author is not an architectural historian, and if architectural styles enter in they do so in order to illustrate the social position and cultural ambitions of their first owners; if the names of landowners, developers, architects, and builders occur it is to explain the shifting economic strategies by which field after field surrendered to bricks and mortar; and if dates are cited from time to time it will be to show that these local strategies – like those of modern University planners – could always be defeated simply by the arrival of yet another period of national economic stringency.

The *Walks* were often written in haste against the deadlines of fortnightly publication. They have now been revised for a wider readership in this more permanent form, and also somewhat re-ordered. Although the style of a travelogue has been maintained, the circumnavigation now begins and ends at the steps of the Parkinson Building, our most public face, accessible to visitors by public transport from the city centre, and where the University's public information bureau is to be found.

Neither the lay-out of the campus nor the chronology of its red brick buildings permit a straightforward progress from A to Z. The necessarily erratic route may be followed from the map. For those readers, on the other hand, who prefer to embark upon the *Walks* in a seated position in front of a fire, numerous visual aids have been provided, in accordance with the precepts of modern university teaching methods, which will at least enable them to follow the route in their mind's eye.

On the steps of the Parkinson Building history is revealed to a keen observer underfoot and on all sides. Underfoot, in the granules and exposed fossils of the Portland stone it is counted in millions of years. In the surrounding townscape of Woodhouse Lane the time-scale contracts, and there is very little in sight that cannot be explained in terms of events from the last two hundred and fifty years.

THE PUBLIC HIGHWAY is indeed the oldest feature. In origin it was a lane from the village of Leeds leading no further than the extensive Town Moor which Leeds shared with the hamlet of Great Woodhouse, providing grazing commons, stone quarrying and the occasional working of low-grade open-cast coal. The centre of the small hamlet of Great Woodhouse lay along the north-eastern side of the Moor on the opposite side of the road from the University, near the present Woodhouse Street. The ground alongside Woodhouse Lane was of better quality than the Moor and was enclosed into fields for agriculture, probably in the later Middle Ages. The ownership and shape of these fields were important factors in determining how the nineteenth-century streets and terraces were to lie: the houses of Blenheim Terrace, for example, almost facing the Parkinson steps, represent one such field.

From 1754, when it was turnpiked, Woodhouse Lane became part of a new thoroughfare to Otley, Wharfedale, Skipton, and Kendal, replacing the older main road which reached Otley via Burley and West Park. There were turnpike riots in Leeds, and opposition to the tolls would have been stronger if the turnpike gates had been placed at the Old Town Bar where Woodhouse Lane left the Headrow at what is now the pedestrianised area adjoining (the former) Lewis's Department Store. Were the road still a turnpike, the Parkinson steps would be just outside the toll-free zone, for the first turnpike gate and keeper's lodge were set at the limit of mid-eighteenth-century town development, very near the present traffic island and flower bed in front of the Parkinson steps. The quasi-turnpike and keeper's lodge (in the form of a traffic barrier and security booth) to the south of the island is a more modern invention for the monitoring of University-bound traffic but older members of the University will remember that the flower-bed marks the site of a different survivor of the pre-motor age, a stone trough for the watering of horses who found the gradient of Woodhouse Lane as trying as an overweight professor who hurries back from town with a shopping bag in time for a two o'clock lecture.

Neither before nor after 1754 did housing development along Woodhouse Lane present a continuous frontage. The merchants who purchased roadside fields in which to build their new out-of-town residences found the southern side, with the possibility of drawing-room views across the Aire valley, the more attractive. The area of the Visitor's Car Park behind Emmanuel Church results from the demolition of one of these, Ridge House, built for the merchant John Hebblethwaite in 1790; and the furthest development with its drive just by-passing the turnpike gate was Earl Cowper's Woodhouse Lodge (c.1797) which was demolished in 1927 to make room for the then Mining (now Mineral Sciences) Building. The northern side of the road was less favoured, and its development was later and more sporadic, as the surviving buildings show. In 1795 the owner of the field now occupied by Blenheim Terrace was advertising it as salubrious building ground 'with most beautiful, picturesque and extensive Prospects' but no Hebblethwaite or Cowper responded to the siren song, and

WOODHOUSE LANE, BLENHEIM TERRACE, TRINITY ST DAVID'S CHURCH, THE 'CORTEN STEEL' TOWER OF BROADCASTING PLACE AND, IN THE FAR DISTANCE THE 'STUDENT RESIDENTIAL' AND OFFICE BLOCKS TOWARDS THE CENTRE OF LEEDS.

thirty years elapsed before house building began there; and although Blenheim Terrace was in the event built in a superior style its individual houses did not match in cost or social standing the larger detached merchants' houses that faced them across Woodhouse Lane. Demolition has swept these latter houses from sight although surviving houses of their type will be encountered in other parts of the campus later in these *Walks*. Blenheim Terrace on the other hand is largely intact and it merits closer examination.

The 'View from the Steps' has remained largely unchanged except for the far distant views of the tower blocks towards the city centre, most notably the 'red rust' Corten Steel tower of Broadcasting Place. But we should realise that had Chamberlin, Powell and Bon's Development Plan come to full fruition there would have been no Blenheim Terrace nor even any steps! In their revision of the plan (1963) these architects refer to the 'formidable' steps confronting the visitor from Woodhouse Lane and proposed a ground level service road *directly in front of the Parkinson Building* with a mere platform or forecourt at the entrance to the building above. It is curious that this singularly horrific proposal never seems to have been commented on, nor even noticed, by any committee or member of the University. The whole of Blenheim Terrace, and all the buildings as far as the Inner Ring Road (save the BBC Building – now part of Leeds Metropolitan University's Broadcasting Place) were to be replaced by 'landscaping' (trees and shrubs) and a new Vice-Chancellor's Lodge, in octagonal form, where the HSBC Bank now stands, raised up on pilotis and linked to the University by an over-bridge. Woodhouse Lane was planned to be re-aligned further east crossing the Inner Ring Road by the (now) never-used bridge.

Finally, before we descend the steps, we should notice that the plinths to each side are empty. They were intended by the architects to be surmounted by statuary: a standing figure with two smaller ones on one side, and a standing figure and one seated on the other. Doubtless they will always remain empty, for, apart from the matter of funding, who should be represented? Not chancellors or vice-chancellors, nor even distinguished professors, for like students they come and go and are forgotten.

> *Note: The photograph accompanying Beresford's description involved a certain amount of visual licence: the viewpoint was and is not from the steps at all but much higher up, from the window of a room adjacent to the Council Chamber.*

*INCLUDING THE UNIVERSITY BUILDINGS
ALONG WOODHOUSE LANE*

We descend Woodhouse Lane as far as Blackman Lane. Retracing our steps, we can better appreciate the chronology of the building development of Blenheim Terrace. Then, continuing as far as Clarendon Road we observe the dislocated sequence of buildings on our right and the long range of University buildings on our left.

DESPITE ITS NAME this Terrace is not contemporary with the Battle of Blenheim but, like the latter street-names of Cavendish, Clarendon, Eldon, and Cromer, shows its builder seeking the cachet of a name with an aristocratic connection. In Bath, Bristol and the West End of London units of street-frontage development had been called 'terraces' since the early eighteenth century: in Leeds the unitary form of an elegant terrace had been known since Park Row (1767), South Parade (1776), Park Place (1778), and East Parade (1780), but all these West End developments, it will be noticed, avoided the use of the word 'terrace'. The first rows of houses in Leeds to be named terrace did not in fact have a roadside frontage, for Brunswick Terrace (1819/24) occupied a long, narrow field with its shorter side abutting on North Street, the road from Leeds to the Harrogate turnpike. Lyddon Terrace (1825) (*page 59 below*) also lay within a field, turning its back on to the nearest road, Kendal Lane (the later Clarendon Road). Blenheim Terrace therefore was the first roadside terrace in Leeds, less elegant than Park Row or Park Place but having the advantage of cheaper land which permitted substantial front gardens behind which the long façade could be appreciated, as it still can on a summer evening or at a week-end when no cars are parked in these terrace gardens.

In 1824 the much-advertised roadside field called New Close at last found a purchaser in the solicitor T. E. Upton, who was very active in amassing working-

NUMBERS 2, 3 AND 4 BLENHEIM TERRACE SHOWING THE UNIFORMITY OF THE PARTIALLY RESTORED FAÇADES.

class housing in Burley Road and elsewhere. The years 1824 and 1825 were heady years of speculative optimism and saw much extension of industrial, public and residential building in all parts of Leeds: the collapse of the boom of 1826 brought correspondingly serious bankruptcies. Sir Walter Scott's insolvency was hastened by his involvement as a sleeping partner in an unlucky attempt to create a New Leeds just inside Chapel Allerton at Louis Street and Cowper Street, and we shall encounter many half-achieved projects of 1824 and 1825 in other sections of these *Walks*. In Blenheim Terrace the stop came in 1826 when only three houses had been built at the north end of New Close, the present numbers 19 to 21. Number 19, shows what a fine façade all these houses once had; but the added rustic porch and bow-windows of number 20 show no feeling for the period and the unfeeling transformation of number 21 (Austick's University Bookshop) puts it high on the list of any competition for the ugliest building adaptation within the campus. Its present occupiers cannot be blamed for the sins committed when the house was a private school, but the Austick brothers must have had to subdue their aesthetic to their commercial sense when they bought it. The next development, in 1830, was the erection of number 3 near to Blackman Lane and the remaining space was filled between 1834 and 1839. At the lower end of the Terrace, some garish signs apart, the original façades have been less molested and the full beauty of the original design can be appreciated, the longest line of houses of their period to survive in Leeds and miraculously preserved from being tenemented and degraded in the inter-war years by their occupation as offices.

The curve of the turnpike road cut into the ground at the north end of the Close, leaving much less room for buildings with gardens, and it was 1861 before number 24 was built, 1867 before the fanciful line of fairy-tale towers reached number 27, and 1881 before the line of houses and shops was completed to the junction with Blenheim Walk. When houses of this Victorian period become scarcer and more prized we may regret that the banks have also shown that they have more money than sense in debasing these façades with the standard money-shop fronts and signs.

We continue the Walks *by proceeding from Blenheim Terrace towards Woodhouse Moor.*

The short length of Eldon Terrace shows that it was built as a unity, but its plain façade, the small house-size and its architectural style set it far distant in time and social ranking from Blenheim Terrace where a sizeable number of the first occupants had been officers' widows and other annuitants. Eldon Terrace dates from 1824 and the adjoining Eldon Place from 1833. The former Eldon Wesleyan Chapel of 1890 is now derelict. The surviving slogans and murals of the interior derive not from its occupancy by the Wesleyans, the School of

NUMBER 21 BLENHEIM TERRACE 'THE UGLIEST BUILDING ADAPTATION WITHIN THE CAMPUS' (BERESFORD) – BUT WHICH NOW HAS A CERTAIN PERIOD 'ART DECO' CHARM.

Chemistry or the University Library book stack, but from the depredations of a libertarian 'alternative' school in the early 'seventies.

St Mark's House, 186 Woodhouse Lane (the St Ann's Community hostel), *c*.1830 is the last survivor of a villa tradition on the north side of the turnpike although it once had a twin at the demolished number 188. Between Eldon Chapel and St Mark's House was a field with only a short side abutting on Woodhouse Lane, so that street development within it had to take the form of building plots set along a frontage at right angles to the main road, making Kingston Terrace. The incomplete Kingston Terrace is a fine example of the risks that went with building investment. It was begun in 1826 by the members of a terminating (or subscription) building club but was abruptly terminated in an unintended sense by the general commercial crash and the departure of the club's treasurer to America with the funds. The abruptness is indicated by the adjoining vacant plots and the incongruous nineteen-thirties suburban house built right against the Terrace end. The great stone gate-posts that guarded the (still private) unsurfaced road survive, although the keeper's lodge has gone. Along-side are the odd gate posts (phallus with a rosette) that once guarded the private road to Eldon (or Highfield) House (1834) and Ridge House (1802), both now demolished.

Beyond St Mark's House St Mark's Street gives a view of the Anglican church erected in 1823/25 with a Parliamentary grant, one of the three in Leeds intended to improve the morals of the infidel working classes in the new industrial

THE PACKHORSE AWAITS ITS DROVER, TURNED TO STONE.

districts. In Woodhouse the industry and industrial housing of that day were concentrated on the Meanwood Valley side of the church and the first working-class houses near Woodhouse Lane did not arrive until the cemetery (*page 43 below*). The public house now called the Eldon was built in 1839 as a victualler's and beerhouse, then given the name the Cemetery Tavern: no doubt the refuge of mourners after funerals across the road – although perhaps scandalising the nearby Methodist chapel in St Mark's Street, erected in 1831 and now occupied by Civil Engineering postgraduates. Number 192 and the stone-built number 194, sacred to fish and chips, also date from 1839. A row of four shops ended at number 200 which still has fragments of its original wooden doorcase of 1834. The Pack Horse pub has a longer history than the Eldon, probably catering for the pack-horse drivers on the turnpike. It appears on a plan of 1796 and was advertised in 1799 as 'old and well-established' and may be the building on the Moor edge shown in Jeffreys' map of 1767/70, although from the exterior it is a Victorian re-building, possibly after the auction sale of 1868. The pack-horse over the door is badly in need of attention from the Royal Society for the Prevention of Cruelty to Sculptured Animals: perhaps a collection to restore the poor creature to its former rude health could be taken from animal lovers at the bar?

Since Beresford wrote, Blenheim Terrace has been much improved by cleaning and the restoration of the brickwork, door-cases and windows so that we can now appreciate more fully the beauty of the original design – despite the almost total loss of front gardens. Except of course Austick's, now Blackwell's, bookshop, one of the first built (1826) group of three houses. But even here the passage of time has lent a certain charm to the vaguely art-deco exterior of the 'ugliest building adaptation within the campus'. The façades of the banks (Nos. 24 and 27) have also been improved. But what is now most striking is how the proliferation of cafes and coffee bars has added what might be called a 'Parisian zest' to this upper end of Blenheim Terrace.

Of all the *Walks*, that from Blenheim Walk towards Woodhouse Moor has seen the greatest changes. Eldon Place and the Wesleyan Chapel have now gone and of Eldon Terrace only two houses survive, incongruously situated in front of the bow-fronted façade of Eldon Court, a building wholly out of scale with its neighbours and vying for dominance with the University buildings opposite. That planning permission should ever have been granted for such an intrusion is a matter of extreme regret. Then we come to Kingston Terrace, set at right-angles to Woodhouse Lane and, further on, St Mark's House (now numbered No. 1 St Mark's Avenue) which now houses the Yorkshire College of Music and Drama. It was never St Ann's Community Hostel; this was housed in the villa on the opposite side of St Mark's Avenue – surely the 'twin' which Beresford described as 'demolished'?

Then, passing the Quaker Meeting House we come to St Mark's Street. The Methodist Chapel has gone, to be replaced by a singularly dismal red-brick block and the Eldon (which once boasted a tiny, cosy, tap-room behind the Woodhouse Lane frontage) has been extended to take over the grocery shop which stood at one corner of Spenceley Street; on the other corner of which was the fish and chip shop, fondly known to generations of students as Sweaty Betty's, or simply Sweats. Mahmood's restaurant and terrace now occupies the site of Sweats and the row of four shops, not a trace of which remain.

We now stand outside the Packhorse, below the now garishly painted sculpture. We should notice, on the far corner of Clarendon Road, the former Woodhouse Library (which incorporated a police station) an attractive late nineteenth-century 'domestic style' building, now given over to drink rather than knowledge.

We now repeat our walk from Blenheim Terrace to notice the great range of Portland stone University buildings on the other side of Woodhouse Lane – buildings which represent unequivocally the public face of the University. This era in the University's development was ushered in by Sir James Baillie, Vice-Chancellor from 1924 to 1938. In 1925, following a building appeal, an architectural competition was held which was won by the firm of Lanchester, Lucas and Lodge and which was formally adopted by the University in 1927. What we now see is but a small, and very much diminished, fragment of that prize-winning scheme. It included a formal sequence of 'Beaux-Arts' classical buildings along the south side of University Road (close to where Beech Grove Terrace, the University Union and University House now stand) and designed to 'look down' on the City of Leeds like the buildings of the Acropolis looking down on Athens. Of that grand sequence only the Arts Block was completed (in the 1960s) and in a much reduced architectural language. H. V. Lanchester, the senior partner of the practice, was a leading architectural planner of the late nineteenth and early twentieth centuries: he planned the Civic Centre at Cardiff and made major contributions to the planning of Imperial Delhi. However, following his retirement the detailed designs for the buildings we now see fell to the junior partner, Thomas Arthur Lodge. He envisaged that the buildings would be of red brick with substantial Portland stone dressings but in 1928, during the construction of the first building to be erected (the former Mining Building), the University made the significant decision to use Portland stone wholly for the Woodhouse Lane facing façades (with brick behind). Then followed from 1932, the Chemistry/Physics building, planned to face the (former) Mining Building across a little triangular 'square'. These however only served to emphasise the rawness of the red brick exterior of the Library (begun in 1930) and perhaps it seemed that in 1935 the centrepiece of the scheme – the grand colonnaded entrance to the University, reached by a flight of steps and flanked on either side by statuary – would never by completed. However, in 1936, following a substantial donation by a former student, what we now know as the Parkinson Building was commenced in 1939 but not completed until 1951, following the interregnum of the war years. It is a magnificent achievement and the tower, the crowning landmark of the University, now features in the University's 'logo'. Those of us who like to look for precedents may recognise, in form if not in scale, the tower of Los Angeles City Hall.

Perhaps it was inevitable that the 'Beaux-Arts' classicism of these buildings could not be continued into the post-war era. The Engineering and Houldsworth Buildings, which complete the sequence along Woodhouse Lane, designed by Allan Johnson, a junior partner in the firm, and built in the late 1950s – early 1960s, are stripped of all classical allusions. And although they may be said to represent the swan-song of the Portland stone era, they are not without merit – particularly in the uniform fenestration of Civil Engineering (1960), Mechanical Engineering (1961) and Electrical and Electronic Engineering (1963). Moreover, Johnson's fibre glass mural above the entrance to Mechanical Engineering, executed by Alec Dearnby, is a striking and wholly successful decorative feature.

In 1956 Dr Lodge announced his retirement and from 1959, with the appointment of the firm of Chamberlin, Powell and Bon, the University embarked on a wholly different phase in its building development.

THE PARKINSON BUILDING: THE UNIVERSITY'S PUBLIC FACE ON WOODHOUSE LANE.

THE BOLD FIBREGLASS RELIEF SCULPTURE ABOVE THE ENTRANCE TO MECHANICAL ENGINEERING.

THE FORMER WOODHOUSE LIBRARY 'GIVEN OVER TO DRINK RATHER THAN KNOWLEDGE'.

In this Walk we retrace our steps from Clarendon Road and the Moor, continuing
past the Parkinson building and descending Woodhouse Lane as far as the Inner
Ring Road. Then, observing the buildings on the opposite side of Woodhouse Lane
to Blenheim Terrace, we arrive at Hillary Place, at which our Walk terminates.

NO OLDER BUILDING has survived the determined onslaught of the 1950s which
made room for the Central Boiler House and the line of applied science
departments. As their varied exteriors show, public funds flowed more freely
than in the 'seventies; and within, social historians will note that a Professor of
Civil Engineering could study hydraulics in his private loo. Among the casualties
in this demolition was the old manor house of Great Woodhouse, but the
presence of the cemetery had inhibited villa development on this side of the road
and limited later development to working-class terraces with some interior
courtyards behind them which became subject to clearance orders before 1939.
A short access road brought hearses past the monumental mason's yard to the
cemetery entrance, but our entrance on foot will be later in the *Walks* from the
southern side near the Agricultural Sciences Building (*page 49 below*).

We pass the Parkinson steps and go towards the city.

The landscape is dominated by the two churches, one Anglican and one
Nonconformist. Emmanuel dates from 1880 and Trinity from 1900: they are
thus comparatively late arrivals, and the now open space of the car park between
them represents the house and grounds of the merchant John Hebblethwaite who
built Ridge House here in 1790 and lived here for nearly fifty years until his
death in 1840. His heir, his great-nephew, John Hillary Hebblethwaite, had his
own residence and interests in Huddersfield and therefore set about developing
this part of this inheritance as the red brick of Hillary Place.

Before perambulating Hillary Place, which begins near the traffic lights, there is a small group of red brick houses and shops which survive from a larger area demolished for the Inner Ring Road and once centred on Fenton Street. The Street commenced in 1842; like the Fenton Hotel (1853) on the Woodhouse Lane frontage it took its name from Isabella Fenton whose friend Henrietta Strickland bought a group of fields here in 1840 and in 1853 built the house which later became the Fenton Hotel. No houses of this period survive from Fenton Street itself but the shops on the Woodhouse Lane frontage are all converted houses of 1847; the former chemist's shop was built in 1857.

The Strickland territory ended at the shop now occupied by the Department of Archaeology (a house of 1845); and the post office on the facing corner (1857) and its neighbour, which also houses part of Archaeology, bring us back to the edge of the grounds of Ridge House and J. H. Hebblethwaite's projects for his inheritance. Ridge House itself was let to the banker J. W. Scott for his family and four resident servants; in the grounds a smaller villa was erected between 1844 and 1847 for another banker, George Hyde. JHH must have been fond of the initial letter 'H' since he named this house Hope Villa, renamed Ridge House Hillary House, gave Hillary Place as a name for a new street that he planned across the southern part of its grounds, and named the first house in it Hopewell House (1847). Hopewell House still stands on the Woodhouse Lane frontage where Hillary Place began but Hope villa was sold in 1900 for the building of Trinity Church.

Hopewell House was substantial: it was built for Henry Littlewood, a coach proprietor who operated from a yard in Briggate. He did not remain long, and by 1853 was living in Chapeltown, then a leafy suburb. In the census of 1861 the occupant of Hopewell House was Henry Pritchard, flax merchant, and the household included three resident servants, one a page-boy, that is only one fewer than at the much larger Hillary House.

Hillary Place was designed as a cul-de-sac with a private drive to its rear, the present road between the buildings occupied by the University Student Health Service and the School of Education. No houses were built on its north side, the grounds of Hillary House and Hope Villa, until the caretaker's house for Trinity Church in 1901. The development on the south side was, as elsewhere, sporadic. The earliest two houses cannot now be seen, since liquid nitrogen is now delivered to the Physics laboratories where callers (from 1884) could leave their cards on Alderman Bateson and his wife, or where the postman could make a special call at their neighbour, the Leeds postmaster himself. (The Chief Constable at this time was just down the road at 153 Woodhouse Lane, on the corner of Fenton Street, a house to which the University has recently restored a domestic façade.)

Number 5, the next to be built, still stands as part of the Education complex. It was first occupied in 1853 by John Crofts, a partner in Donisthorpe and Co., wool merchants and manufacturers at Larchfield Mills, Hunslet. It served as the home of vicars of Leeds from 1890 until its purchase by the University in 1926. For many years it housed Geology before becoming part of the Education complex. The former number 1 (now, appropriately enough, part of the Department of Theology and Religious Studies) was built as Gordon Villa in

1859 for William Myers, wine and spirit merchant, although the faint traces of inscriptions on the downstairs window mark the later occupancy by Laverty's, 'manufacturers of objects of religious' (actually Roman Catholic) 'devotion'. Number 2, of the same date, has been demolished to give egress from the car park. Numbers 6 and 7, which abut against number 5, were built between 1859 and 1861, possibly by the architect Elisha Backhouse who was the first occupant of number 6. The interiors of this group of massive houses are more interesting than their exteriors.

At this time J. H. Hebblethwaite was also developing Hillary Street (from 1856) and Vernon road (from 1860) but no houses remain in these streets. In 1860 he sold a plot of land from the northern end of the gardens of Hillary House to the vicar of Leeds for the building of Emmanuel Church, although it was another twenty years in fact before operations began. Hillary Place itself was also slow to be completed: there was a ten-year interval before number 8 (1870) and number 4 (1872) were built. Number 4 is demolished but number 8 forms the cornerpiece with Cavendish Road, the opposite side of which had begun to come into existence (also in Hebblethwaite land) between 1859 and 1861. The grandiose corner house was built for T. R. Harding, card, comb and steel pin manufacturer of the Tower Works, Globe Road; but his son, Colonel T. W. Harding (who designed City Square), was the first occupant in 1870.

HILLARY PLACE: GRANDIOSE AT THE CORNER (1870), SOLID AND PLAIN BEHIND (1859/61).

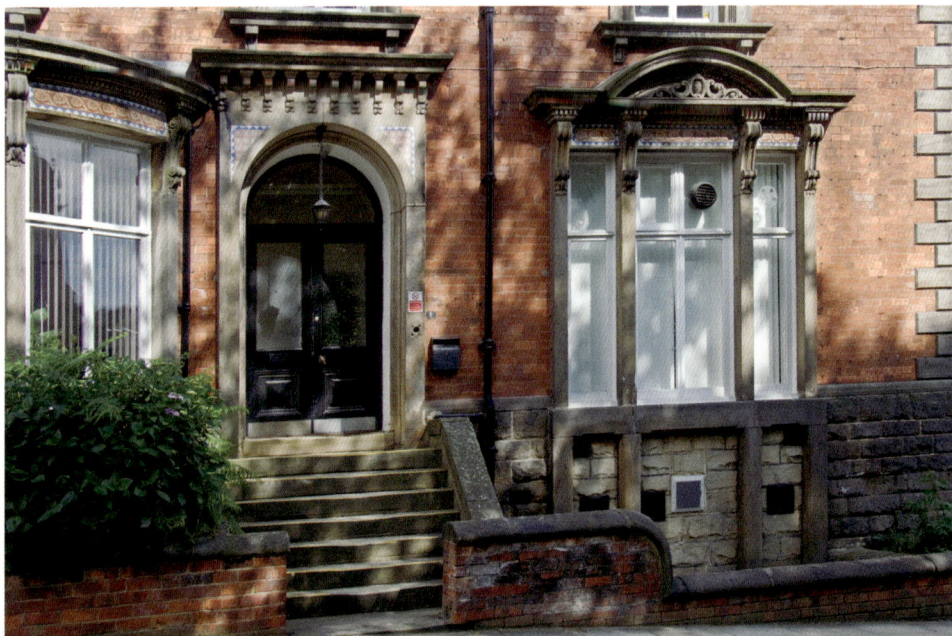

NO.1 HILLARY PLACE: DETAIL.

The Anglican church, 1876-80, by the architects Adams and Kelly was re-modelled by Halliday Clark in 2004 for the University Chaplaincy. Trinity St David's Church, 1899-1901 by G.F. Danby, has undergone a less appropriate transformation – as a café-bar and nightclub.

Beresford's perambulation begins, in effect, at the Inner Ring Road, opposite the dominant corten-steel towers of Broadcasting Place. It is difficult to follow on the ground because we have to imagine the sites of buildings and gardens long-submerged under later developments – Fenton Street, for example (no street sign) once continued across the line of the Inner Ring Road. Nor does Beresford mention Lodge Street, at the corner of which is the Department of Archaeology on one side and the former Post Office (an early casualty of 'rationalisation') at the other. This building of 1857 is now occupied by a Department with the curious title 'Inter Disciplinary Ethics Applied'. The former chemist's shop just below the Fenton pub (No. 159 Woodhouse Lane) is now 'Strawbs' bistro (formerly Strawberry Fields). As we progress towards Hillary Place along Woodhouse Lane we pass the offices of the Leeds International Piano Competition (No. 169a), the Instituto Cervantes (No. 169), then, further on, Hopewell House itself (No. 173) – which looks rather less substantial than Beresford describes. No trace of inscriptions of 'the objects of religious devotion' in the windows of former No. 1 Hillary Place (175 Woodhouse Lane) now remain except for a monogram 'ILS' in a staircase window. The Physics 'deck' and the loading-bay are of course horrible intrusions in Hillary Place. The numbering of the houses in Hillary Place is difficult to follow. The first block after the Physics loading bay with the large round-arched doorway is numbered 5-9, then we have No. 6, then a blocked doorway, then No. 8 as Beresford describes at the corner with Cavendish Road. Where therefore is No. 9?

As an entrance gateway to the University campus, Cavendish Road has been much enhanced by the Marjorie and Arnold Ziff building which in effect counterbalances the visual domination of the E.C. Stoner building.

ALTHOUGH WITHIN THE barriers of the University traffic control, Cavendish Road and Hillary Place, with their pavements, walled front gardens and surviving coach houses at the rear, manage to preserve the appearance of true streets; even though nearly half the original length of Cavendish Road has been submerged under the glass and concrete of the Physics-Administration Building which boasts Europe's longest corridor. Fortunately the imaginative scheme devised by Geoffrey Wilson, Planning Officer in the 'sixties and 'seventies, for the conversion of the Presbyterian Church (1879) to the Clothworkers' Centenary Concert Hall has left the original entrance intact. On a Sunday morning the empty street allows the ghosts of the unco' guid Celtic exiles who formed most of the congregation in 1879 to come down the steps unobserved and walk to Hillary Place where pedestrianisation has forced their grooms to wait respectfully by the pawing horses, impatient for home and their Sunday lunch of hay in the coach houses of Headingley Hill and Far Headingley.

It was on a November Sunday morning in 1947 that I first caught sight of Cavendish Road on my way to being interviewed by an appointing committee. These committees were then held in a long-demolished house in Beech Grove Terrace (which we will be moving to later – *pages 31–36 below*), but afterwards A. J. Brown (himself then only in the second of the thirty-two years of his service as Professor of Economics) led the new recruit back to his room in number 6 Cavendish Road to discuss future duties.

THE SCHOOLMISTRESS OF THE HOUSE? KEYSTONE FROM FRONT DOOR OF
MISS MATTERSON'S SEMINARY, NUMBER 10 CAVENDISH ROAD (1875).

A HEAVY STONE PORCH WITH INEDIBLE FRUIT, NUMBER 6 CAVENDISH ROAD (1863).

It was not, I think, untypical of current disdain for the abundance of Victorian domestic architecture then making up the suburbs of English cities that I should have felt some disappointment that I was not going to work in the smart Portland stone part of the University (then not very extensive). I had read my Bruce Truscott *Red Brick University* and was not surprised by red brick lecture theatres and a red brick Great Hall: but these were purpose-built for a provincial university. Was there not something of second-class citizenship in working in a second-hand red brick house?

In recent years visitors have sometimes commended the University's good sense in preserving the remains of a Victorian street as the avenue to its modern buildings. It is difficult to re-capture the actual mood of the early days of Charles Morris's Vice-Chancellorship (*c.*1950) when there was competition to get oneself demolished; and a renewed feeling of second-class citizenship when the more fortunate were elevated to the Portland stone palaces between the cemetery and Woodhouse Lane. Number 6 Cavendish Road, where the Department of Economics had been since 1932, had a very low place in the demolition queue, awaiting if not the Second Coming then at least the coming of some benefactor with funds for a giant new concert hall and auditorium which was the designated occupant of this area in the Chamberlin plan.

It is also chastening to recall how oblivious of building history was that young lecturer in economic history thirty years ago, being too exhilarated that particular morning to notice that there were no houses numbered 2 and 4 in Cavendish Road. Later wisdom explains the open space to the north, then tennis courts and now the Social Sciences research terrapins, as a deliberate sterilisation. It had been bought for that purpose in 1852 by the owner of the end nine houses in Beech Grove Terrace who wished to preserve the open view southward when Hebblethwaite's building plots looked like being taken up.

In fact there were no takers for this Hebblethwaite land until after a second sale plan in 1859, dividing the land in smaller lots for contiguous houses rather than the detached villas of the 1852 project. In both schemes the tapering shape of the field forced the front gardens to become shorter as one moved down the hill: and, as we have seen at Blenheim Terrace, with shorter gardens the class of house deteriorated. Newcomers may not easily realise that until the building of Physics/Administration there were ten more houses below the Presbyterian Church and nine on the other side below Student Health; nor that the cul-de-sac was once closed by number 25a, alias 27, the surviving but distant house now occupied by Chinese Studies. The Chinese and Mongolian inscriptions on its doorway are necessarily all Greek to me: but they are unlikely to read (as they might truthfully do) 'the house of Alfred Hoggard, builder and master joiner, erected for his own occupation in 1883'. This endpiece was not the last building in the road: in 1883 all the (now demolished) houses below the Church had still to be built, and the opposite side was not completed before 1892 with houses also now demolished.

Cavendish Road had thus taken thirty-two years to complete. In 1860 Joseph Horsfall, a machine-maker and partner in the Victoria Foundry, purchased Lots 70 and 72 of the Hebblethwaite grounds and proceeded to erect the present numbers 3, 5 and 7 on the east side of the newly laid-out road. At the census of

1861 he lived in the end house, number 3, with his wife, two sons, and two resident servants; the tenant of number 5 was William Cooke, a wallpaper manufacturer; at census time numbers 7 and 9 were incomplete. On completion Horsfall sold number 7 to Henry Lampen, clerk to the Poor Law Guardians and the Superintendent Registrar for Leeds, being thus responsible for the whole Leeds census of 1861; number 9 was built on land purchased from Hebblethwaite by A. O. Martin, an account-book manufacturer in Briggate.

The original unity of this quartet of houses of 1861 can still be faintly discerned on the bricks to the right of their doorways where painted numbers 1, 2, 3, and 4 have not been wholly obliterated by time. This numbering had to be changed after building commenced on the other side of the road in 1864, the Leeds custom demanding odd numbers on one side and even on the other; and when a house was built on the corner plot with Hillary Place in 1870 its front door had logically to be number 1, Cavendish Road and the original number 1 then became number 3.

The first house on the western side was built for Jonathan Pulleyn, like Martin a manufacturing stationer. Although having something of the appearance of a terrace house from number 8 being built hard against it two years later, Pulleyn's house was of a superior class to those opposite. Besides its heavy stone porch with inedible fruit, its double-front bay windows and decorative ceramic tiles, the below-stairs kitchens were extensive. Number 8 was purpose-built as a ladies' seminary for its proprietress, Miss Elizabeth Matterson, so successful that in 1875 she sold number 8 and built a larger school next door. The interior of number 10 has been modified during University use, but its exceptionally wide staircase to all floors, including the basement, must have been designed for young ladies to process in double file. The stone lady over the door may be Miss Matterson, gorgonized.

In 1878 the foundation stone of the Presbyterian Church was laid, on a site still separated from Miss Matterson's by an empty plot. This church was designed by J. B. Fraser and opened in 1879. Number 12 may conceivably have been intended as its manse.

The largest house in the road, the present-day number 1, is bisected internally, with a second entrance on the Hillary Place side. Its first owner, the engineer Colonel T. W. Harding (*see page 15 above*), lived in the Cavendish Road half from 1870 to 1877 and had tenants in the other half which has no less grand a doorway, staircases and fittings than if it had been part of an original design: yet the Hillary Place doorway, set back and beyond the line of quoins, has the air of an afterthought.

In the site plans for the Hebblethwaite building plots in 1852 the western limits were marked as 'the estate of Mrs Lyddon' or 'Mrs Lyddon's trustees', and it is to the Lyddon estate that these *Walks* now lead. The boundary between the Hebblethwaite and Lyddon estates is not difficult to follow on the ground: it is represented by the backs of the Cavendish Road houses lying north of the Concert Hall and facing the South Library. Mrs Lyddon's fields were eventually covered with more densely-packed houses than any that we have so far visited; but virtually all have been demolished for such buildings as the South Library, Mathematics, Earth Sciences, the Senior Common Room, and the Roger Stevens

THE (TRUNCATED) CAVENDISH ROAD, SHOWING THE PRESBYTERIAN CHURCH AND MANSE (1878), EARLIER HOUSES BEYOND (1875, 1864 AND 1863) AND THE ENFOLDING ARM OF THE MARJORIE AND ARNOLD ZIFF BUILDING.

THE WESTERN SIDE OF CAVENDISH ROAD (EVEN NUMBERED HOUSES) LOOKING TOWARDS THE SCHOOL OF MUSIC.

Lecture Theatre. It is fortunate that the scattered survivors are the earliest buildings, erected between 1821 and 1825, but tall University buildings prevent them being seen from the back of Cavendish Road, and they must be visited one by one.

The Physics-Administration Building is now named the E.C. Stoner Building, commemorating Edmund Stoner, FRS, a former distinguished Professor of Physics. Whether or not it boasts Europe's largest corridor is a matter of debate – it bears no relationship of course to the 'Corridors of Power' described in C.P. Snow's 1964 novel of that name! The Clothworkers' Centenary Concert Hall – the former Presbyterian Church of the 'unco' guid Celtic exiles' – designed in 1870 by J. B. Fraser was converted in two stages: first in 1974-5 when Beresford was writing and again in 2004 by Harrogate Design. This firm also designed the extension to the School of Music (2003) which replaced a truly hideous bunker-like concrete lecture theatre block – a building which Beresford, with perhaps too great a sensitivity, does not notice. His autobiographical sketch, as the new recruit to a lectureship in economic history in 1947, is evocative of the spirit of the time. The hoped-for relocation of the Department of Economics (and Social Studies) in a smart new Portland stone building never materialised. Instead it was long after (1978) re-housed in the last building to be erected under the Chamberlin Plan – a building never itself completed as can be seen today by the stark gable-end facing and linked to the Marjorie and Arnold Ziff Building. I can imagine a future new recruit to Economics, unappreciative of the finer points of concrete brutalist architecture (as Beresford and his colleagues were of Victorian domestic architecture), hoping, in turn, to be re-housed and to work in a finely-proportioned Victorian drawing-room!

REFLECTIONS OF CAVENDISH ROAD IN THE MARJORIE AND ARNOLD ZIFF BUILDING.

The School of English now occupies Nos. 6-10 and the School of Music No. 12 (which yet retains the air of a Presbyterian Manse). The extension, built on the site of the concrete 'bunker' (in the gap between No. 10 and No. 12), in its materials and scale, fits in well with the streetscape. It is curious that the 'young lecturer in economic history' did not also notice the gap between No. 10 and No. 12. Was it also to preserve the view of the houses in Beech Grove Terrace?

The houses Nos. 1-9 on the opposite (east) side of the road are now occupied by University administrative departments – but the remnants of a notice-board, directing students to the appropriate Health Service entrance, may still be glimpsed at No. 3. The surviving but distant house (No. 25a) on the far side of the E. C. Stoner Building, no longer exists. But the greatest change to Cavendish Road is the erection, on the site of the 'Social Science terrapins', of the Marjorie and Arnold Ziff Building (architects Farrell and Clark), the sinuous curve of which, like a great enfolding arm, terminates the vista at the top of Cavendish Road.

The backs of the even-numbered (west side) Cavendish Road buildings which mark the boundary between the Hebblethwaite and Lyddon Estates, now face a pleasant landscaped area, enclosed on the far side by the Edward Boyle (formerly South) Library. Boyle, a patron of the Arts and Music, was a former Vice-Chancellor (1970–81) and prior to that a Minister of Education.

In the late eighteenth century there was a group of fields between Woodhouse Lane and the hamlet of Little Woodhouse (page 82 below) that belonged to the wealthy merchant, Wade Preston, whose father and grandfather had been mayors of Leeds, and who died unmarried at his house in Scarcroft in 1789. His heiress was his sister's daughter, Julia Silly.

BY 1805 JULIA Silly had houses at Boston Spa and at the more fashionable spa at Bath. According to an affidavit which he swore in 1847, J. S. Morrish, her Leeds property agent, was called to her house at 2 Queen Square, Bath on the night of 26 October 1805, which he remembered as the night when the news of Nelson's death reached Bath. His purpose was to make a copy of a plan which she possessed showing her uncle's nineteen-acre estate in 1739. This plan, which is now with the copy and affidavit among the University Bursary deeds, showed seven fields of irregular shape and all unbuilt upon.

If she had intentions to develop the estate in 1805 they were unfulfilled; but after her marriage in 1807 to Captain William Lyddon she returned to Leeds to live in Park Square and began to exploit the building potential of these fields, which could be realised only if access carriageways or roads were driven into them. In 1821, with Morrish as architect, a small detached Georgian house was built in the centre of the area (Preston Lodge), and two south-facing terraces were commenced, one (Blundell Place) at the south and the other (Preston Place) at the north. Clay was dug on the site, bricks were made in a coal-fuelled kiln near Blundell Place and surplus bricks sold to other builders. Julia's husband was closely involved in the financing of these operations, mainly by issuing 147 IOUs over his single signature to stone-masons, plasterers, ironmongers, marble fireplace makers, plumbers, glaziers, and carpenters. 'She used frequently to joke about Captain Lyddon, a very kind husband, being a brickmaker', Benjamin Clarkson, stone merchant, told the Court of Chancery in May 1837.

By the end of 1824 only three terrace houses were in fact erected in Preston Place and three more in Blundell Place, but undeterred by the two incomplete terraces Julia invested a further £3950 in the heady atmosphere of the boom year 1825 by purchasing fifteen acres of land to the west of her uncle's estate, almost doubling its area.

The surveyor Henry Teal was commissioned to prepare a map to further the expected sales which has survived among a solicitor's collection now in the City Archives. It shows the street we now know as Lyddon Terrace laid on the western side with two plots backing on to Kendal Lane (later Clarendon Road) already sold and a second road (the later Mount Preston) also with three plots sold.

With 1826 came the same commercial crisis which brought Blenheim Terrace to a halt, and the remaining Lyddon building plots remained empty. Julia Lyddon died in 1828, and a fate nearly as bad as bankruptcy lay in wait for the estate, for no sooner was her will read than two lawsuits were initiated in Chancery: one between her two great-nephews, Cloberry Silly Woolcock and Frederick Silly Parkyn, over the validity of a death-bed codicil to her will; and the other between her trustees and her husband over the latter's claim for £1815 worth of bricks which he had supplied for building Preston Lodge and five other houses. An interim settlement was reached after sixteen years – actions in Chancery were not speedy – but only two months before Captain Lyddon's own death, and Lyddon vs. Woolcock was to linger in Chancery until 1853. The lawyers at least did well out of the estate, and nothing could be more appropriate than the Faculty of Law having its rooms and library in Lyddon Terrace (*page 64 below*); and it will now be realised whence came the affidavits about the news of Lord Nelson's death arriving in Bath, that copying of maps, and the details of Captain Lyddon's promissory notes to the tradesmen and craftsmen who fitted out the new houses.

What of these houses? Since these *Walks* are concerned only with surviving houses we may ignore Blundell Place which has long given way to the old Dental Hospital and visit next the two developments that commemorated her uncle's name: the detached house, Preston Lodge, and the uncompleted terrace Preston Place (later re-christened Beech Grove Terrace).

Preston Lodge – the 'Lodge' was a modest diminutive – can be appreciated even from the outside, for three sides of it are untouched by its conversion to University use by extensions at the rear. Its south-facing porch had a clear view over the fields towards the Aire valley in 1821, but the three auction sales of building plots in 1845/47, following the interim settlement in the Lyddon Chancery suit, transformed this view. For just over a century the stature of Preston Lodge was diminished by the houses densely packed into this building plot, but the recent clearances have re-opened a southern vista across Willow Terrace Road to a new sports field. Some moment of penury in the long progress towards the Chamberlin plan for the campus halted its demolition, and the genteel poverty of the University's building fund may now save it forever. It is a plain house, straight out of the same Georgian textbook as Springfield House (*page 75 below*) but on a reduced scale; within, the original stairs and the ceiling cornices of the main rooms can still be seen.

PRESTON LODGE (1821), AN EARLY DEVELOPMENT OF THE LYDDON ESTATE.

NUMBERS 5, 7 AND 9 WILLOW TERRACE ROAD: A LATE DEVELOPMENT OF THE LYDDON ESTATE (1865) AND (RIGHT) THE FORMER LEEDS CHURCH MIDDLE CLASS SCHOOL (1875).

Before passing from Preston Lodge to Preston Place there are three neighbouring houses to the east which deserve a moment's attention: 5, 7 and 9 Willow Terrace Road. They stand on Lot XXVII in an auction sale of plots from the Lyddon estate in 1851, the fourth in the long series, although they were not built until 1865. They now house the photography section of the Audio-Visual Service. From the Sports Hall side, on Willow Terrace Road, their original front doors can be seen blocked, and with their bay windows these three houses were superior to any of their demolished neighbours in this street. The two isolated public buildings to the east derive from later purchases still: an annexe of Leeds Polytechnic occupies the former Leeds Church Middle Class School of 1875, and the University Department of Physical Education has a practice ski slope and other athletic altars in the church built for the Swendenborgian sect in 1884.

To return to 1821 and the earliest Lyddon houses in Preston Place (later re-named Beech Grove Terrace) it is necessary to return past the Physics/ Administration (E.C. Stoner) Building towards the Great Hall and the University Union. The three surviving Lyddon houses adjoin the Union gates and back on to the Great Hall.

This is the Court of Chancery; which has its decaying houses and its blighted lands in every shire; which has its worn-out lunatic in every madhouse, and its dead in every churchyard; which has its ruined suitor, with his slipshod heels and threadbare dress, borrowing and begging through the round of every man's acquaintance; which gives to monied might, the means abundantly of wearying out the right; which so exhausts finances, patience, courage, hope; so overthrows the brain and breaks the heart; that there is not an honourable man among its practitioners, who would not give – who does not often give – the warning, 'Suffer any wrong that can be done you, rather than come here!

This passage, taken from the first chapter of Charles Dickens' *Bleak House* well describes the effects, upon its victims, of the interminable proceedings of the Court of Chancery. The lawsuits which followed Julia Lyddon's disputed will were, as Beresford points out, only finally settled in 1853 (the year that *Bleak House* was published in book form) – a period of twenty-five years. The victims of that saga – the Lyddons, the Woolcocks and the Parkyns – are long forgotten – so also are the lawyers who were of course the chief beneficiaries. But, as Beresford shows, the consequences of those lawsuits can still be recognised 'on the ground' in the dislocated building development of Lifton Place and Lyddon Terrace (Chapter X).

We now make our way past the spine of the E. C. Stoner (Physics/ Administration) Building to Preston Lodge on Willow Terrace Road – the earliest building (1821) to be erected on the Lyddon Estate. The rear extensions have gone but the façade has been given a uniform coat of white/grey stucco which contrasts strongly with the red brick of the Department of Food Science which has been built alongside. The 'southern vista' across Willow Terrace Road which Preston Lodge briefly

NEW JERUSALEM CHURCH OF 1884.

enjoyed following the demolition of the closely-packed houses, has once again been blocked by erection of 'The Edge' – the University's building for 'Fitness, Sport and Well-Being'. How permanent, one may ask, is 'The Edge' and how many years will pass until the southern vista of Preston Lodge is restored once more?

LEEDS CHURCH MIDDLE CLASS SCHOOL 1875 (NOW YORKSHIRE AND HUMBER
POSTGRADUATE DEANERY) AND A DISTANT VIEW OF THE E.C. STONER BUILDING.

The neighbouring three houses (5-7 Willow Terrace Road) now house the Department of
Occupational Health and one of the front doors has been restored to its proper use – the other two
have been very elegantly disguised. But how forlornly isolated does this terrace of three houses
appear, a modest group of buildings linking them to Preston Lodge would do much to restore the
streetscape of Willow Terrace Road.

The Leeds Church Middle Class School of 1875 (note the datestone in the side gable) now
houses the HQ of the 'Yorkshire and Humber Postgraduate Deanery' and the 'New Jerusalem'
church of 1884 of the Swedenborgian Sect appears to have lost its ski-slope.

It is worth emphasising that Beech Grove Terrace takes its name from Beech Grove – the long demolished house which was the first home of the Yorkshire College when it moved here from its first site in Cookridge Street in 1876 (see Ch. VII) and of which the only visual record is the drawing in the Bilbrough sketchbook (pages 34–35).

THE TERRACE AT Preston Place had only three of its houses erected when first the commercial crisis and then the litigation following Mrs Lyddon's death postponed development for thirty years, building commencing again in 1850 and being completed by 1866. By a coincidence it is only these later houses that have been demolished leaving the original numbers 1, 2 and 3 as isolated as they were while the Woolcocks and Lyddons fought in Chancery. Like their demolished neighbours, they housed the University's first overflow after 1918 into rented (and subsequently purchased) private housing. I cannot be the only member of the University who remembers being interviewed by an appointing committee in one of these now-demolished houses and being apprenticed to committee membership and University politics in another of them.

The three original Lyddon houses were integrated at the time of the expansion of the Department of History after 1948 before it moved into the New Arts Building, and one unhappy consequence of that integration was the blocking-up of the front door of number 2 so that even the recent renovations and restoration have left the trio with an odd appearance, three divided by two making for a rather vulgar fraction, so to speak. It is ironical that this disfigurement took place when Asa Briggs, author of *The Age of Improvement*, held our Chair of Modern History; although it must be admitted that widespread demolition elsewhere on the campus had not then given these buildings their present scarcity value.

Indeed the buildings have always been rather an embarrassment to a succession of University architects. Unlike back-to-backs, elegant terrace houses could not face both ways, and Preston Place was designed to look south to the sun. It did not have coach-houses at the rear, for the depth of the field in which it was built was small, but there were sunken area basements (for the damp souls of housemaids to sprout in), wash-houses, WCs, coalhouses, and the like. One disadvantage of the site chosen for the University's first buildings in 1877 was that the cloisters of the Textile Department and the later baronial glory of the Great Hall faced straight into these back yards which the University did not at that time own, and distinguished visitors stood in the porch of the Great Hall to gaze at the dustbins while they awaited their Rolls-Royces. There is a well-known photograph of these humble outbuildings covered with bunting and loyal subjects waiting for Edward VII and his Queen to leave the Great Hall. Only recently has this back area had its domestic origin camouflaged and a main entrance for Plant Sciences created, leaving the front doors to open – if they can be opened – only to the lawns and the new stone piazetta [*sic*].

In the census of 1841 each of the three houses had room for three resident servants and something of their character when first erected can be seen from the contents of the middle house as revealed in a *Leeds Mercury* advertisement of 6 May 1822 (p.33).

THE THREE REMAINING HOUSES (NUMBERS 1, 2 AND 3) OF BEECH GROVE TERRACE (FORMERLY PRESTON PLACE), COMMENCED IN 1825.

PRESTON PLACE, WOODHOUSE-BAR
VALUABLE & MODERN FURNITURE, CHINA, GLASS &c. &c

Messrs. LUMB respectfully announce that they are instructed to offer for SALE by AUCTION (by order of the Proprietor, Mr. Hernaman, who is Removing his Private Residence), on the Premises of No. 2, Preston Place, near Woodhouse Toll Bar, on Monday and Tuesday, the 28th and 29th of June, the Elegant, Modern and Valuable DRAWING and DINING ROOM FURNITURE, comprising Twelve handsome Rose Wood Chairs, with loose Cushions; Elegant Sofa; a Pair of beautiful Rose Wood Card Tables; Rose Wood Sofa Table; Pair of Foot Stools; Window Curtains, with Gilt Cornices, elegantly fitted up with Drab Moreen and Light Blue Silk Borders and Fringe; Ten and Two Armed handsome Mahogany Fluted Chairs, with loose cushions; Mahogany Patent Dining Tables, with Three Leaves; Elegant Mahogany Side Board; Mahogany Loo Table with Claw Feet; beautiful Mahogany Cabinet Book Case; Fire Screen; Brussels Carpets; Fenders; Fire Irons; Hearth Rugs; Window Curtains, elegantly fitted up with Crimson Moreen and Silk Fringe; Foot Stools, &c. &c. Also the excellent BED ROOM FURNITURE, including handsome Mahogany Four Post and other Bedsteads, with Hangings and Window Curtains to match; Prime Feather Beds; Hair, Flock and Wool Mattresses; Carpets; Mahogany Ward-Robe; Pier, Swing and other Glasses; Painted Wash Stands, Dressing Tables and Chamber Services; Mahogany and Painted Chests of Drawers, &c. &c. Various Rich Cut Glass; beautiful China and Earthenware in Dinner, Desert and Tea Services; Vases, Ornaments, &c. Hat Stand, Passage Lamp; various Kitchen and Brewing Utensils, &c.

The Sale to commence each Day at Eleven o'Clock, and Catalogues, which may be had of the Auctioneers, 19, Cheapside, Leeds, will be ready for Delivery on Friday the 25th Instant.

Messrs. LUMB respectfully inform their Friends and the Public, that the above Furniture having been supplied by the first Manufacturers in the County, is of a very superior Description; – is in the best possible Condition; – and the Whole is the genuine Property of the Vendor.

John Hernaman, a bookseller, had been the first occupant of number 2, and good advice about furnishing could have been obtained from his neighbours on either side, for Mr Mouncey at number 3 and Mr Kendell at number 1 were the partners in Kendell and Co, Mill Hill, 'upholsterers, cabinet makers, hair seating and curled hair manufacturers', perhaps the 'first manufacturers in the county' of the advertisement.

A different insight into number 1 at a later period is afforded by a remarkable documentary survival. From 1855 this house, the westernmost of the terrace, was occupied by the family of John Brooks Bilbrough (who died in 1885), manufacturing chemist in Briggate. His eldest son, Alfred, was a patron of the arts and a benefactor of the City Art Gallery; a younger son, John, was a skilled amateur artist. Two sketch-books containing work by these brothers have been presented to the Leeds City Archives Department by a descendant of Alfred's executor. They are made up mainly of domestic scenes executed by John Bilbrough between 1879 and 1892, the kitchen and the drawing room now transformed to the uses of Plant Sciences; and – relevant to the next section of the *Walks* – drawings and paintings of two houses that he could see from his windows at a time when the Yorkshire College of Science was erecting its first buildings to the north of his back door.

THE CAMPUS AS SEEN BY JOHN BILBROUGH IN 1886. A VIEW NORTHWARDS
FROM HIS HOUSE TO 'MR LAWSON'S – BEECH GROVE, BUILT 1796, PURCHASED
BY THE YORKSHIRE COLLEGE IN 1876 AND DEMOLISHED FOR THE BUILDING
OF THE GREAT HALL A WEEK AFTER THIS SKETCH WAS DRAWN ON 5 JUNE
1886.

THE WALLED YARD NORTH OF THE BILBROUGH HOUSE IN JANUARY 1884,
DOMINATED BY THE TREES IN THE GROUNDS OF BEECH GROVE HOUSE (MR
MARCH'S), BUILT IN 1799 AND SURVIVING AS THE SOCIAL SCIENCES
INSTITUTE. THE WAREHOUSE AND COUNTRY HOUSE OF THE MERCHANT
ABRAM RHODES WERE STILL STANDING (CENTRE). ON THE EXTREME RIGHT
CAN BE SEEN THE BRAND NEW TEXTILES BUILDING.

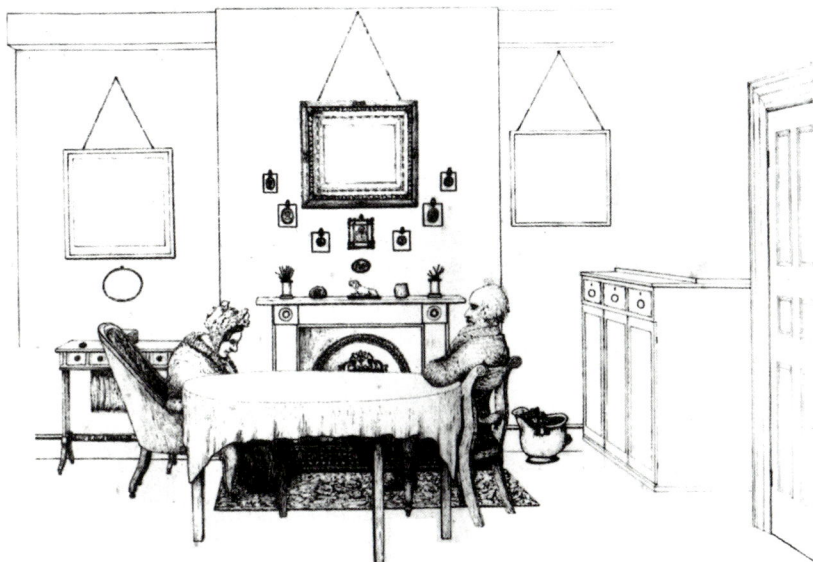

UPSTAIRS AT NO.1 PRESTON PLACE. A DOMESTIC INTERIOR (OF 1885?) WITH JOHN BROOKS BILBROUGH AND HIS WIFE. AN UNFINISHED SKETCH BY JOHN BILBROUGH.

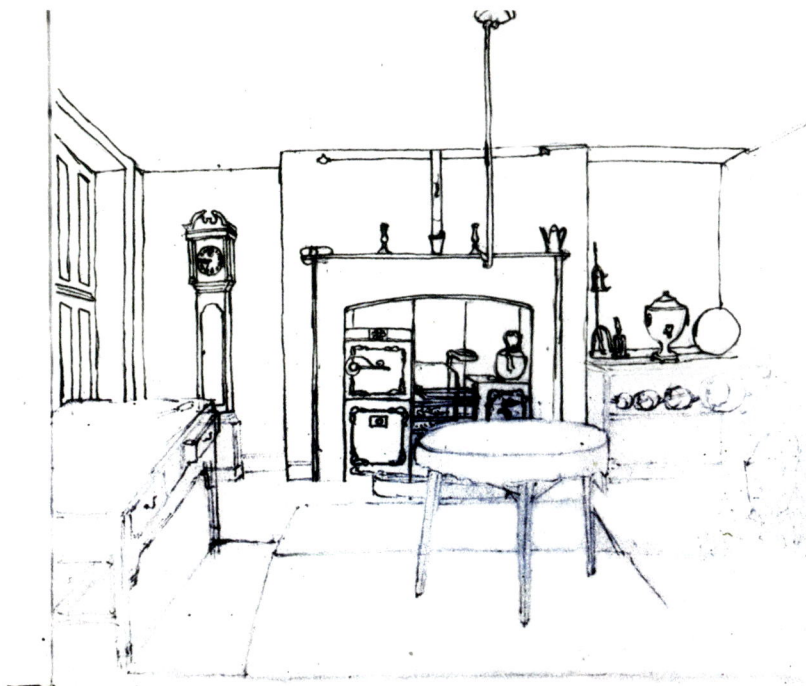

DOWNSTAIRS AT NO.1 PRESTON PLACE. THE BASEMENT KITCHEN SHOWING THE CAST-IRON RANGE AND FURNISHINGS IN THE ALCOVES EACH SIDE. AN UNFINISHED SKETCH OF 1892 BY JOHN BILBROUGH.

UNIVERSITY HOUSE AND (LEFT) THE UNIVERSITY UNION — A CONTINUATION OF THE RED BRICK BUILDING TRADITION

The dustbins upon which the 'distinguished visitors' used to gaze have long gone and the rear elevations of Beech Grove Terrace (now called Botany House) have been much improved with 'planters'. Furthermore, the lower part of University Road has been landscaped with stone paving – providing at last a dignified frontage to the University buildings.

The new stone 'piazzetta' which Beresford refers to is the stepped area, with covered walkways, which leads to the Economics and Social Sciences Building and the 'Spanish steps' which continue past the Edward Boyle Library to Chancellor's Court.

Although the Students' Union and University House do not directly face the front elevation of Beech Grove Terrace, it is instructive to compare the use of red brick in the façades. The former buildings were designed by J.C. Procter (architect, with F.L. Charlton, of the gatehouse and central block of Devonshire Hall on Cumberland Road (1928) – a building very much in the Oxbridge College tradition). The Students' Union was completed in 1939 and University House in 1955 but constitute, in effect, one seamless terrace.

This Walk, essentially a continuation of that in Ch. VI, takes us to the earliest red brick buildings of the Yorkshire College along College, later University, Road and now pedestrianised for most of its length. But not long before the time that Beresford was writing the '56 bus' trundled its way along here!

THE DETACHED MERCHANT houses of the 1790s so far encountered were built in fields adjoining Woodhouse Lane so that carriages could easily approach along a short private drive. The supply of such convenient fields on the popular south side of Woodhouse Lane was limited, and the two merchants who built Beech Grove and Beech Grove House in 1796 and 1799 had to purchase fields lacking direct access to the turnpike.

Beech Grove was built for Benjamin Murgitroyd who took out a fire insurance policy in May 1796 for a house 'unfinished but intended for the occupation of its owner'. At the same time he laid out a private carriage way along the south side of his field, probably where a footpath already led directly from the south-east corner of Woodhouse Moor (that is, near the present Henry Price Building) to join Woodhouse Lane by the horse-watering trough already mentioned (*page 2 above*). It was Beech Grove with its outbuildings and its gardens that the Yorkshire College of Science purchased in 1876 with the intention of moving from its original temporary rented premises in Cookridge Street.

John Bilbrough made drawings of this house and its demolition in 1884 to make room for the Dyeing Department, and also sketched at this time another house of the same character and period which lay to the west and was rather confusingly named Beech Grove House. This house has not been demolished: it stands between the University Union and the Great Hall, and has been known to generations of students as Education House. It originated in 1799 when

Abram Rhodes, a leading cloth merchant and exporter in the town, bought two contiguous fields called White Cross Closes, coming to an agreement with his neighbour at Beech Grove to share the private carriageway from the turnpike. Like other merchants whose buildings we shall encounter later, Rhodes built in the same field as his house a group of warehouses and workshops for handicraftsmen as well as a malt kiln. These are shown to the north of his house and to the west of Beech Grove on a plan of 1830, when the industrial buildings at the rear were in contrast to the lawn, shrubbery and ornamental pond that had been fashioned from White Cross Close on the southern side of the houses, and Mr March's 'park' was one of the few subjects in the Bilbrough sketch book to be treated in colour.

In 1810 Rhodes turned to factory production, building mills at Woodhouse Carr, and in prosperity left Beech Grove House, first for a Leeds suburb (Roundhay) and then for a country estate (Wold Newton). In 1840 his trustees sold Beech Grove House to a representative of another stage in the industrialisation of Leeds, the iron founder and machine maker John Ogden March, apprentice and then partner of Matthew Murray at the Union Foundry, Dewsbury Road. The house still had the malt kiln and warehouses alongside it, but three smaller houses had been inserted between them. March did not need the textile warehouses and they continued to be rented to the Rhodes firm.

BEECH GROVE HOUSE (1799) (NOW THE SOCIAL SCIENCES INSTITUTE) WITH A LATER SIDE PORCH IN 'VICTORIAN NORMAN' STYLE.

THE GREAT HALL BY ALFRED WATERHOUSE 1892-94.

SCHOOL OF DESIGN: EXTENSION TO THE SPINNING DEPARTMENT AND TOWER BY
PAUL WATERHOUSE, 1911.

As the neo-Norman porch on the eastern side and the bow-windows show,
there have been alterations to the house, and the iron gates appropriate to an
iron founder signify a line of approach moved from the original private
carriageway to take advantage of Beech Grove Terrace. The domestic interior of
Education House is particularly attractive, although it is dominantly of the iron
founder's period rather than the cloth manufacturer's. Yet there were once
proposals to demolish the house, and the late W. E. Tate led a one-man
preservationist campaign (not unconnected with his ambition for it to house his
museum).

The house seems to confer longevity. The Department (now School) of
Education has been there longer than anyone can remember or indeed intended,
but not so long (yet) as the Miss March who came there with her father in 1840
as a little girl of three, eventually inheriting the house, to die there in 1925. She
therefore saw the whole development of working-class streets to the south, the
arrival of the Yorkshire College, its extensions and its gradual occupation of
private houses in adjacent streets. It was her wish that the University should
acquire her estate intact among this urbanisation, and fortunately for us her
legatees were remote, well-settled and prepared to sell.

ukpaperbackshop

PAPERBACK SHOP (AMAZON)

UNIT 22-26 HORCOTT IND ES
HORCOTT ROAD
FAIRFORD GLOS
GL7 4BX

Deliver To:

JOHN ALAN WILLIAMS
4 PINFOLD DRIVE
ECCLESTON
ST HELENS
MERSEYSIDE
WA10 5BP
UNITED KINGDOM

Ordered By:

John Alan Williams
4 Pinfold Drive
Eccleston
St Helens
Merseyside
WA10 5BP
UNITED KINGDOM

Qty	ISBN	Title			Price	Total
001	9780900741715	WALKS ROUND RED BRICK				

Despatch Summary:	Despatch Date:	21/08/2014	Total Items:	1
	Delivery Method:	PBS Standard	Goods Total:	
PK: 7721	Total Parcels:	1		
	Delivery Charges:		Reference:	026-7610129-026

Please tick the reason why you are making a return.
( ) Damaged   ( ) Faulty
( ) Wrong Item ( ) Other

Please confirm the option required.
( ) Refund   ( ) Replacement

If necessary to return, please send (enclosing reason for return) to:

GB RETURNS PAPERBACK SHOP
UNIT 22
HORCOTT INDUSTRIAL ESTATE
HORCOTT ROAD
FAIRFORD
GL7 4BX

17694904

The Leeds Improvement Act of 1865 extended the private carriageways of Beech Grove and Beech Grove House westwards to the Moor, and made a public road to replace the footpath over a cabbage patch to a ginnel and turnstile that Miss March remembered as the way to the Moor from her father's house. The thoroughfare acquired the name College (and later University) Road: until an archway was built at its Woodhouse Lane end in 1958 to link the Parkinson and the New Arts Buildings, and that part of the road pedestrianized, it carried much traffic, including the 56 bus. The central portion is now also pedestrianized and landscaped, although the road surface and kerbing are partially preserved.

This is the route to be followed towards our next objective, passing under the arch which has the brightly-coloured arms of the University's benefactors, the Clothworkers' company, on its western side. The motto 'IN GOD WE TRUST' was until recently qualified by an illuminated sign declaring a limited headroom of 33 metres. Readers of smaller stature may pass through and turn right beyond the School of Geography to seek the steps and narrow opening which lead through the high boundary wall into St George's Fields, the Leeds General Cemetery of 1833. The low-built superstructure of the School of Geography, it should be noted, stands on a complex foundation; somewhere underneath lies part of Rhodes' malt kiln of 1799 which survived there until it was bought by the Yorkshire College in 1900 and converted to a refectory.

It is not easy, from Beresford's description, to identify the precise location of Beech Grove (built 1796) – the first permanent 'home' of the Yorkshire College of Science and which was demolished in 1884 to make room for the (former) Dyeing Department, now Colour Chemistry. No photograph of the house is extant and John Bilbrough's sketch only gives us a partial glimpse. Perhaps this might be the occasion for the placing of a blue plaque or the raising of an obelisk.

Beech Grove House (1799) now houses the Social Sciences Institute and its setting has been transformed by the recent landscaping all around – from the newly paved University Road to the North, the open 'piazza' to the East (which provides a visual link to Beech Grove Terrace) and, most significantly, the newly-lawned area to the South, with trees and benches and which provides a visual link to the University Union and University House. This new urban setting re-creates, in a sense, the open aspect which Beech Grove House enjoyed when it was newly-built in the green fields of the Estate.

From our viewpoint in the newly-landscaped area in front of Beech Grove House we have an uninterrupted view of the red brick 'Collegiate Gothic' University buildings along University Road, representing the first phase in the University's building development. In 1877, three years after the founding of the Yorkshire College, the Council made the momentous decision to invite Alfred Waterhouse to become University architect. Waterhouse was the most celebrated English architect of public and university buildings of his day. His Manchester Town Hall was just being completed and his Natural History Museum in Kensington was then under construction – surely two of the greatest buildings of Victorian England. His university work included Pembroke and Gonville and Caius Colleges in Cambridge, Balliol College in Oxford, Owens College in Manchester and Liverpool College.

Waterhouse planned a long range of buildings along the north side of the carriage-way which led from Woodhouse Lane to the Beech Grove and Beech Grove House Estates which became known as College (later University) Road. With substantial funding from the Clothworkers' Company the first building was erected in 1879-1880 for the Department of Textiles (now the School of Design). It stands on the west side of the present Clothworkers' Court, its gable end of red brick with dressings of Spinkwell sandstone facing College Road is enlivened with a commemoration plaque and sculptured teasels (symbolic of cloth-working). Further west the long cloister-like façade hid the weaving sheds behind. Then, following a substantial benefaction by Edward Baines, Chairman of the College Council, the Baines Memorial Wing was built in 1881-85 east of, and separated from the Textiles building (Beech Grove and its grounds lay in between). The main entrance at the centre of the long façade is accentuated by the stubby tower above and has the date 1883 over the doorway. At the far east end, at the junction with Woodhouse Lane, Waterhouse planned a further extension with a great clock tower but this was never built. Instead, a range of utilitarian buildings were erected, to be demolished in the 1930s to make way for the Brotherton Library.

While the Baines Memorial Wing was under construction a further benefaction from the Clothworkers' Company (1883) provided for the building of the Department of Dyeing, set back from College Road in the grounds of Beech Grove and forming the north side of what was to become Clothworkers' Court – the most pleasing feature of Waterhouse's scheme. The square tower at the north-west corner provided the setting for the crime novel *The Weight of the Evidence* by J. I. M. Stewart, lecturer in English 1930-1935, who wrote under the pen-name of Michael Innes.

Thence there was both a building lull and a major status change: in 1887 the Yorkshire College was admitted as a constituent college of the federal Victoria University and thus became a University College.

Two major schemes were initiated following the accession of the Yorkshire College to the Victoria University: the Great Hall and the new (now old) Medical School in Thoresby Place, close to Gilbert Scott's Infirmary, for which a building appeal was launched in 1890. The Great Hall, with library and reading rooms beneath, was an addition to Waterhouse's original plan and required, at last, the demolition of Beech Grove itself. The drawing (page 34) from the sketch-book of John Bilbrough, an amateur artist, resident at No. 1 Beech Grove Terrace provides the only visual record of Beech Grove shortly before its demolition in June 1886. The Great Hall, begun in 1892 and completed in 1894 with its remarkable staircase of glazed Burmantofts bricks is the grandest of Waterhouse's buildings at Leeds and came in for much criticism at the time for its extravagance. It is curious that in the hall itself appear the intertwined letters 'Y. C.' rather than 'V. U.' since from its commencement, the College had been a constituent college of the Victoria University for some five years!

The last buildings to be erected along University Road are by Paul Waterhouse, Alfred Waterhouse's son. He designed the link building between the Great Hall and the Baines Wing in a quite distinctive 'Arts and Crafts' style (built in 1912) and, to the west of the first Textiles building, an extension for the Spinning Department, terminated by a tower in a much 'freer' gothic style than that of his father and with a commemorative plaque of 1911.

This great range of buildings rapidly became smoke-blackened and their architecture denigrated by later generations of architectural critics. That era is now past and as we pass along University Road we can appreciate them as if they were newly built. Now we pass under the arch (better described as a bridge) which links the (former) Man-Made Fibres building (1954-6, by Allan Johnson) to the extensions of the Paul Waterhouse buildings. Turning around, past the bridge, we still see the object of Beresford's gently mockery: the Coat of Arms and the motto of the Clothworkers' Company. But the motto reads 'MY TRUST IS IN GOD ALONE', not 'IN GOD WE TRUST' – gently mocking Beresford in return for what must have been a lapse of memory.

St George's Fields is a green and partially tree-shaded oasis on the northern edge of the University campus – best visited in May/June when groups of students sit or lie in the sunshine revising for exams; or in autumn when the trees have turned to gold. It is regrettable however that the access routes are so restricted – that leading in from the rear of the Estates building, past loading bays and parked vehicles, is particularly hard to find.

THE HIGH BOUNDARY wall was erected to deter anatomists rather than vandals; but even anatomy students may now enter without fear of the law since the University of Leeds Act 1965 extinguished the few remaining burial rights and permitted the creation of a public open space which has been re-christened St George's Fields. In 1833 this was the name of four closes measuring some ten acres that the directors of the newly-formed Leeds General Cemetery Company purchased from the widow of Colonel St George Dalley of Great Woodhouse Hall.

In the years when the cemetery was in use there were three lawful entrances: the Greek gate-house and the two smaller gates on the west side, one of which survives next to Henry Price student flats. The flats have perhaps the most elevated views of the cemetery, but a perambulation of the whole interior is worthwhile.

As with the Leeds Commercial Buildings and the old Corn Exchange a few years earlier, it was decided to make the design of the cemetery the outcome of a public competition which was won by John Clark of Leeds, beating R. D. Chantrell in the field of seventeen entrants. His Ionic temple façade may have looked back, like his Apollo of Delos gate-house, to the fifth century BC, but the other end of the temple looks forward to modern architecture in maximising the area of plain glass. Stained glass might be expected, but this temple was never a cemetery chapel. The divisions between Dissent and Church of England were

THE GREEK REVIVAL GATEHOUSE TO ST GEORGE'S FIELDS (JOHN CLARK, 1835) AND THE REAR ELEVATIONS OF THE ENGINEERING BUILDINGS.

too deep in the Leeds of the 1830s for there to be any agreement on an interdenominational consecration service; the company's directors who, like its patrons, were drawn from both Church and Chapel, simply avoided the issue. The same sectarian divisions had prevented any agreement on the provision of a municipal cemetery out of the rates in the decade of fastest population growth, 1821/31, and in the decade of the cholera and the national campaigns for sanitary reform, 1831/41. An act of 1842 created the first municipal cemetery for Leeds at Harehills, and there was then a different architectural solution to the conflict of creeds: half Harehills cemetery was assigned to Church and half to Chapel, and each given an identical consecrated mortuary chapel.

The Woodhouse cemetery at St George's Fields, with some five hundred burials a year in this period, was offering only limited relief to the small and overcrowded city-centre churchyards, but it was relief gratefully accepted by the town's middle class. The shareholders' register and the register of burials, which survive in the University's custody among the other company records, are a register of the town's early Victorian élite, including Abram Rhodes and J. O. March of Beech Grove House, the Baineses, the Marshalls, the Bischoffs, the Cawoods, the Gotts, the Fairbairns, the Heatons, the Luptons, the Rawsons, and the Nusseys.

Today the most comprehensive view of the cemetery is from the engineering buildings which overlook the gate-house, the main drive and the porticos of the

THE PATHWAY PAVED WITH STONES FROM 'GUINEA GRAVES', EACH WITH TWELVE INTERMENTS, LEADING TO THE UNCONSECRATED NON-DENOMINATIONAL TEMPLE (JOHN CLARK, 1835).

Greek temple that stands among the lawns and ornamental trees, a landscape designed by Mr Chamberlin after the majority of the monuments had been removed in 1968. A few of special interest went to the City Museum: a limited number were allowed to remain, in rather sad clusters; and the rest were used to create the mounds and hillocks that now give variety and contours to the landscape.

The monuments were erected by the wealthier grave-owners, covering simple graves or family vaults. After competition from the new municipal cemetery in 1842, the company allowed a corner of the cemetery to be used for chapter graves; these lay at the side now overlooked by Textiles and Colour Chemistry and were marked not by monuments but by vertical plain stones, each bearing twelve names. In 1968 the landscape architect employed them in pairs to make footways: when these stones ran out he used modern concrete slabs, which, less defensibly, he had engraved roughly with hieroglyphs to match (but in fact mock) the genuine register of the less affluent dead.

In the years before 1965 the crowded cemetery and its close-packed lines of monuments overgrown with weeds and scrub had given a gloomy outlook for those University buildings along the perimeter. Family vaults were virtually full and burials infrequent. The company's income was small, and the University did not have difficulty in purchasing its shares from owners who had learned to expect few dividends and no capital growth. There was some opposition from local families, although the number of these had been much diminished by the

AUTUMNAL TINTS AND A GRAVESTONE BORDERED PATHWAY IN ST GEORGE'S FIELDS.

THE ANGLER'S MEMORIAL WITH BIRDS AND INTERTWINED FISHES.

post-war street clearances. The University agreed to make a photographic record of each gravestone and monument available to descendants of those interred. This record, now on microfilm, was made personally by the Bursar of the time, Edmund Williamson, whose professional interest in the affairs of the company was matched by his amateur skill in photography.

The original St George's Fields were a little more extensive than the area within the cemetery walls which John Clark laid out to enclose a rectangle. Two

strips of surplus land thus lay outside the wall on the south side adjoining
Rhodes' malt kiln, and they were offered to him. In 1865 his successor at Beech
Grove, J. O. March, used part of this land to erect a quartet of houses as an
investment: in that year the road in front of their garden gates had been made a
public highway. The remainder of the land remained open until it was purchased
for an intended Agriculture building in 1900. March's quartet of houses survive
in University use as numbers 34, 36. 38, and 40 University Road, occupied by
the Institute of Transport Studies and the Careers Service. Since there is now no
University Road it might be appropriate to revert to the name March gave to his
new houses, Beech Grove Place.

Numbers 34 to 40 are a group which show, like their contemporaries in
Clarendon Road and Lyddon Terrace, the use of heavy stone detail coming into
fashion as an embellishment of red brick, an emphasis accentuated by the
blackening of the stonework through age and smoke. There are two stone string
courses, stone bays, stone doorways, and stone steps up over the semi-basements.
The front gardens are generous but the backs severely limited by the cemetery
wall. Who were they designed to attract? All the first occupants were 'of
Independent Means', three of them widows.

The high boundary wall facing Clarendon Road now forms a podium above which rises the long
façade of the Henry Price Flats – a clever and effective design by Peter Chamberlin's partner,
Christoph Bon, who also designed the two remaining 'twin tower' blocks of the Charles Morris Hall.
These student residences, built in 1963-64, are distinctive from Peter Chamberlin's buildings in that
they made use of red-brick, echoing the late Victorian housing which they replaced.

THE ELEVATED 'TERRACE ARCHITECTURE' OF THE HENRY PRICE BUILDING.

The remaining monuments deserve a closer look. There is, close to the temple a statue, much weathered, to Michael Sadler, a Leeds linen merchant and a strong supporter of the bill to limit the hours of work of factory children to 10 hours. Close by are monuments of both architectural and social-history interest: to William Taylor, an angler; to Susannah Darby, wife of 'Pablo Fanque' who fell to her death at a circus in King Charles' Croft; also to Pablo Fanque himself; to Ann Carr, Foundress of the Sect of Female Revivalists; to Charles Hall, V C and Croix de Guerre and to John Holmes whose monument is in the form of the Norman porch of Adel parish church. Close to the Greek gatehouse is the firemen's monument, a late Victorian obelisk, shielded with sculptures of a fireman's helmet and a fire engine.

The concrete slabs 'engraved roughly with hieroglyphics' are no more. They occasioned perhaps the only sonnet, composed by the late Bill Houghton Evans, to appear in the pages of the University *Reporter*.

Lines on the Serpentine Way newly-paved with
Tombstones (true and false) across St. George's Fields

Since all that an unfeeling age interred
Still leaves our headstone harvest incomplete,
Let concrete cuneiform and men inferred
Cipher mock-paupers for our callous feet.

Step firm on collier Jack and seamstress Joan,
Their children culled before they'd time to live:
Cropped, counted, coffined; catalogued in stone:
Troubled no longer, they'll no trouble give.

But these we conjure with a runic text,
(Prometheus' last-born, transcendental heirs)
Might they not their own destiny elect
And, meek no longer, claim what's rightly theirs?

Then, peripatetic deviousness denied,
Might we cross with them, straight to the other side?

Leeds, 1971   W. H. E.

We make our way from St George's Fields to University Road through a narrow opening in the boundary wall at the rear of the former Agricultural Sciences Building (now Geography), the foundation stone of which was laid in 1924. This building has a chequered history. It was designed by Michael Waterhouse (the last of the Waterhouse architectural dynasty) in 1913 and was planned to fit a commanding space on Woodhouse Lane. But when sufficient funds became available it was moved for reasons not documented to a vacant plot on University Road. Beresford asserts, in his article in *Red Brick and Portland Stone* (1975), that in its new position the building is back to front and that 'one can now discern the intended façade only by squeezing against the cemetery wall on its backside'. Whether or not this is indeed the case, readers must judge for themselves by

BEECH GROVE PLACE (NOW NUMBERS 34 TO 40 UNIVERSITY ROAD) AND (RIGHT) A SIDE
ELEVATION OF THE FORMER AGRICULTURAL SCIENCES BUILDING.

inspecting both the cemetery wall and University Road elevations.

Finally we come to the quartet of houses, Nos. 34 to 40 University Road, which now accommodates solely the Institute for Transport Studies. One may perhaps answer Beresford's query 'who were they designed for?' by suggesting that the rooms to the rear elevations, so close to the cemetery boundary wall, were intended to be occupied solely by domestic staff; the south-facing front rooms overlooking the long front gardens being intended as the sole preserve of the their middle-class occupants.

When Beresford was writing, some of the houses here described were not in University ownership and, blighted by the earlier threat of demolition, the area had a somewhat tattered appearance. This, as can be seen on the ground, is no longer the case. Furthermore, the deviation to Chancellor's Court provides a wonderful contrast between buildings on the domestic and monumental scales.

THE FRONT WINDOWS of the four houses just visited look out on to a view that is simply the backsides of the three houses in Lifton Place that had been commenced nearly twenty years earlier. The history of Lifton Place brings us back to the north-west corner of the Lyddon estate (*Chapter V above*).

Construction of houses in Lifton Place was envisaged in the plan issued when the estate first began to emerge from Chancery in April 1845, with two principal streets parallel to Lyddon Terrace and joining Lifton Place at right angles. Together with a short cross-street (the later Cloberry Street) these three developments would have filled the vacant ground between Mount Preston and the extensive gardens of March's Beech Grove. It was the western wall of these gardens that prevented Lifton Place being a through road, as the traffic barrier by University House still indicates.

The naming of Lifton Place was from Lifton on the border of Devon and Cornwall where one of Julia Lyddon's litigious grand-nephews, Cloberry Silly Woolcock, was living; and the cross-street leading back into Lyddon Terrace was given his first christian name. The 1845 sale plan names the street that we know as Cromer Terrace 'Bodmin Street' and Clarendon Place 'Parkyn Street' after the other litigant, Frederick Silly Parkyn, who lived near Bodmin. As it was, only the plots for 5 to 9 Lifton Place and 7 to 9 Clarendon Place were taken up at the 1845 sale. Most of the other plots remained empty for thirty years: by that time even the Chancery lawyers had forgotten the Lyddons and Woolcocks, and the

DOORWAY KEYSTONES AT THE DEPARTMENT OF PSYCHOLOGY, LIFTON PLACE.

developers then turned to the English aristocracy for the rather meaningless prestige names of Cromer and Clarendon. Cloberry Street has almost vanished but its former existence is witnessed by the side-entrance to number 18 Lyddon Terrace (which now houses the Faculty of Law), obviously once a front door.

Of the first three Lifton Place plots, two were taken up (1847/49) by a large semi-detached pair, numbers 5 and 7, and the third by Lifton House, now number 9, which was probably erected by its first owner, the builder Benjamin Burrell. The semis were first occupied by a cloth manufacturer and a commission agent. Of the two houses built in Clarendon Place at the same time, number 9 was occupied by Obadiah Nussey, a partner in Hargreave and Nusseys of Farnley, woollen manufacturers. Less than a hundred yards from the site of his demolished house, Obadiah's portrait hangs in the Textile Department, commemorating his role as protagonist and fund-raiser for the Yorkshire College of Science, the fore-runner of the University.

Lifton Place was completed piecemeal, first by two pairs (number 5 and 7, 1847/49, and numbers 1 and 3, 1856/57), while more than twenty years later numbers 11 to 17 were built by the son of the builder who had erected number 9. The doors, at once Norman and gothic, have keystones carved as human heads, fitting their present tenant, the Department of Psychology.

By 1877 the north end of Lyddon Terrace (Ellerslie Hall) was complete, and building had begun at the southern end of Cromer Terrace. As the uniformity of façade shows, the plots in Cromer Terrace were not developed by individuals but by speculative builders. Mrs Lyddon, who had hoped to grace her estate with long terraces in Lyddon Terrace and Preston Place but failed, would have been pleased to see the uniform terrace style re-appear after forty years of single plot-by-plot development of Lyddon Terrace and Mount Preston.

A first row of ten identical houses was erected on the west side of Cromer Terrace by the builder, George Whiteley, between 1861 and 1864, their large basements making them virtually four-storey houses.

Whiteley left his property on his death to George Hutton, also a builder, and Hutton was responsible for the row of eight houses on the east side of Clarendon Place (numbers 16 to 30), begun in 1881/82 and distinguished by white brick courses and elaborate patterned bricks in string courses, friezes and doorways.

CROMER TERRACE: A SPECULATIVE DEVELOPMENT OF 1877 AND A REASSERTION OF THE CLASSICAL STYLE OF A UNIFORM TERRACE.

The same elements reappear in the façade of seven houses on the opposite side of the Place, built in 1883 (numbers 19 to 31), though two customers rejected his pattern-book doors for their own choice.

To the south of Clarendon Place only two houses remain from demolished streets, 'Roseneath' and 'The Abnalls'. This pair is of the same date as numbers 16 to 30 Clarendon Place but are vast, baronial houses and their lowest level so little below the ground as hardly to deserve the name of basement. Although no plaque commemorates the fact, 'Roseneath' was built for Joseph Hepworth, the pioneer clothing manufacturer.

At 'Roseneath' we are only a few yards from the side of he University hall of residence which inadvertently commemorates Mrs Lyddon in its name. Its building history is complex for, apart from the University's own addition, an original simple house of 1826 was enlarged and altered by the Quaker brush manufacturer Joseph Armistead, who bought it in 1844. It had been built on a Lyddon plot for another industrialist, one Thomas Boyne, the tobacco manufacturer who named it Virginia Cottage in deference to the source of the tobacco leaf. The bow-window of the room, now the Warden's study, was added by 1865 and in 1872 the house was bought by Dr T. C. Albutt who sold it to the Yorkshire College in 1902. Armistead had created a walled garden around the enlarged cottage but as early as 1887 Dr Albutt sacrificed the western part to sell off plots to George Hutton who then completed Cromer Terrace by erecting numbers 10 to 20 (1889/90) repeating many of the architectural motifs of his earlier houses in Clarendon Place but without basements, and confined at their rear by the remaining Albutt garden.

LYDDON HALL: TO THE RIGHT VIRGINIA COTTAGE (1826) AND TO THE LEFT THE SUBSTANTIAL LATE VICTORIAN ADDITION.

ELLERSLIE HALL AT THE CORNER OF LIFTON PLACE AND LYDDON TERRACE

Under the Chamberlin Development Plan of 1960 and its revision of 1963, all the buildings in this area, including Lyddon Terrace, were earmarked for demolition. A new University residential area was planned consisting of 'Double' and 'Triple' Halls of Residence, 'Commercial Buildings' and even 'Staff Housing' – in short the type of residential accommodation that only fifty years later would be seen as largely inappropriate to the needs of students in the twenty-first century. Charles Morris Hall, consisting of two tower blocks and the now-demolished womens' spine block (Mary Ogilvie House) was an example of a 'Triple' Hall of Residence.

CHANCELLOR'S COURT WITH THE STEPS LEADING TO THE EDWARD BOYLE LIBRARY AND,
ABOVE, THE AERIAL WALKWAY OF 'RED ROUTE'.

So we are doubly fortunate in that, as Beresford points out elsewhere, it was only the University's penury that saved this area from demolition. Subsequent cleaning and restoration, both of the buildings and landscaping of the paved areas, have ensured that it has remained a delightful domestic-scale enclave within the University campus. Apart from this, we may note only a few changes to the functions and naming of the buildings themselves. In Lifton Place Nos. 1-3 are now called Lifton Villas and Nos. 5-7 are called Lifton Studios. The Department of Psychology still occupies Nos. 11-17 (Beresford does not speculate as to whether the four keystones carved as human heads were representative of actual persons). Then, to complete this north side of Lifton Place, are the new (1970) buildings of the Psychology Department, again in red-brick and neatly arranged around a little square. The traffic barrier by University House has gone, to be replaced by bollards leading to the newly-landscaped 'Pedestrian Priority Zone' faced on one side by University House and the Union and on the other by the Man-Made Fibres building (look up and see the sculpture by Mitzi Cunliffe) and Beech Grove House (the Social Sciences Institute – see Walk VII).

'Roseneath' and 'The Abnalls' (now 5 and 7 Cromer Terrace) are described in Walk X, but we should take Beresford's hint and deviate here, first to see Lyddon Hall and then for an overview of Chancellor's Court.

Dr Thomas Clifford Albutt was from 1861 to 1889, the renowned Physician to the General Infirmary at Leeds and it was here that he invented the (short) clinical thermometer in 1866. He went on to achieve greater eminence, and a knighthood, as Professor of Medicine at Cambridge. His residence at Virginia Cottage is commemorated in a little stained-glass window in the dining-room of Lyddon Hall; the entwined letters 'CSA' stand for him and his wife Susan. Albutt was not only a physician, he also moved in literary circles, including that of George Eliot. There is some evidence that she drew on him, at least in part, for the character of Tertius Lydgate in *Middlemarch* – the young aspiring doctor who is keen to exploit, in medical treatment, the scientific discoveries, then being made with the microscope. But here the resemblance to Albutt ceases; Lydgate is thwarted by an inappropriate marriage and George Eliot portrays his later career as a retrenchment from his earlier ideals. The attractive myth that George Eliot wrote part of *Middlemarch* whilst visiting Albutt at Virginia Cottage is contradicted by dates: the first instalment was published in 1871 and Albutt only purchased Virginia Cottage in 1872.

The adjacent residential block of Lyddon Hall is a late Victorian addition. It was originally a womens' hall of residence but for most of its life was a mens' hall in which (one might say) the archaic traditions of Oxbridge Colleges were scrupulously observed. The garden of Lyddon Hall has been largely built-over by the extensions to the University Union building; note in particular the curious 'mound' topped by a pyramidal rooflight. This was the debating chamber (another relic of 1960s planning), now used as a theatre.

We now make our way to the flight of steps leading down to Chancellor's Court. And although it forms no part of Beresford's *Walks*, this great open space, likened in 1960 by Chamberlin, Powell and Bon to the great Oxbridge quadrangles, should not be omitted. To the north, stretching away to the vista of the Corten Steel tower of Broadcasting Place, is the long range of the Earth Sciences and Mathematics buildings and beyond the broad flight of steps which lead up past the Edward Boyle Library to the Great Hall and Clothworkers' Court (Walks VI and VII) is the further long range of the E. C. Stoner (Physics/Administration) Building. To the south are the spine blocks of the

THE LONG FAÇADE OF THE E.C. STONER BUILDING LOOKING FROM CHANCELLORS' COURT TOWARDS THE TOWER BLOCKS OF LEEDS.

CHANCELLORS' COURT: THE ROGER STEVENS BUILDING

Garstang and Manton (Biological Sciences) Buildings and to the west on our right, adjacent to where we stand, is the (former) Senior Common Room Building, denoted by its external staircase. Opposite to us, completing the square, is the Roger Stevens Building (the lecture theatre block), linked to the buildings to the north by an overhead walkway.

Chancellor's Court is the centrepiece of Chamberlin, Powell and Bon's development scheme. There was nothing to match it in University planning of the 1960s and it became the model, in inspiration if not in detail, to the planning of the newly-emerging Universities in the 1960s – 1970s. All the buildings, which we see were listed in 2010 as 'buildings of architectural and historical interest' Grade II with the exception of the Roger Stevens Building which was listed Grade II* – a notable accolade for a building less than 50 years old. Hence we should finally make our way across Chancellor's Court to inspect the interior – the landscaping which we pass is of 1995, an attempt, largely successful, to soften the rigour of Chamberlin's design. The best time to visit is 'in between' lecture periods: we see from the central open space vistas of students ascending and descending the tiers of open staircases. The effect is almost Piranesian!

It is in Lyddon Terrace that Beresford's description of the University campus as a 'free', open-air museum (of social and architectural history) is most evident.

BEHIND THE HEPWORTH house in Clarendon Place there is an open space at present used as a car park, and alongside it the surface of the former Cloberry Street leads westwards to the southern end of Lyddon Terrace.

NUMBERS 9 (LEFT), 11 (CENTRE) AND 13 (RIGHT) LYDDON TERRACE.

This Terrace, it must be stressed, was originally intended to be a single east-facing row and no house on the east side was built before 1870. But since few campus walkers, even dedicated northerners, seem to have a built-in compass needle it may be better not to call the two sides of Lyddon Terrace west and east but left and right, taking up a first stance near the car park and day nursery, having the lawyers, as surely they should be, on one's right side.

Lyddon Terrace, short as it is, has the longest range of dates of any street on the campus (1825/1906) and although its houses were erected over a long period by more than a score of different developers there is a remarkable uniformity imparted by the universality of red brick. With recent cleaning, repainting and restoration it is becoming our handsomest street. But one hopes that something can be done about the sad erosion of the facing bricks on one of its two oldest houses, number 13, and the *Home and Gardens* door-lamp that has sprouted on the Georgian portico of number 11, spawned perhaps from the scarcely less incongruous ones recently given to numbers 15 and 19; the white homestead palings of number 9 are a poor match for the original iron railing of its neighbours; and the students at number 15 should also be told that a rainbow letter box is a little avant-garde within a Georgian colour scheme.

The left-hand side of Lyddon Terrace, the older side, now begins with number 7, for numbers 1, 3 and 5 were demolished a few years ago for no visible purpose except grass and cherry trees. As a schoolboy far from Leeds, hardly conscious of the city's existence let alone its University's, I knew of number 1 Lyddon Terrace as the address of J. P. Inebnit, of the International Voluntary Service for Peace and other good causes.

NUMBERS 37 TO 41 LYDDON TERRACE.

Numbers 7 and 9 were not the first to be built and indeed give a misleading impression of the Lyddons' ambition in 1825. To assess this, one must go on to the majestic pair of houses numbers 11 and 13, built to be let as an investment. They are modelled in red brick but otherwise very like the Bath stone houses that Captain and Mrs Lyddon would have known in their other home. With two large windows on either side of their doorways, they are double the size of the three contemporary houses in Beech Grove Terrace, and indeed as large as anything in Park Square or Park Place in the West End of Leeds. Their social status is measured by their large kitchen cellars and their three storeys. In the census of 1841 number 11 had four resident servants and number 13 had three. Robert Frost, of independent means, was then living at number 11 as a tenant of the Lyddons as he had been ever since it had been built (three of his five children were probably born there) but at the Chancery sale of 1845 he bought the house for himself as well as a plot on the opposite side of the road to preserve his view, and at his death in 1875 he had lived in the house for fifty years.

His neighbour at number 13 in 1841 was William Willock, the collector of stamp duties for the borough and four adjoining wapentakes of the West Riding. He had moved up from Hanover Square between 1830 and 1834, also as a Lyddon tenant, but had left after the Chancery sale. In the auction details of that sale the two front rooms of each house, dining rooms and drawing rooms, were measured at 19 feet by 17 and the back breakfast rooms at 16 feet by 14 ½; in each there were 'four excellent bedrooms with dressing room and water closet' on the first floor, and four bedrooms on the second; there were no attics; at the rear, accessible from what is now Clarendon Road, were two-stall stables and two coach-houses, another sign of the occupant's status.

Land to the north and south of these two houses had been sold by the Lyddons before Julia's death but not immediately built on by their purchasers, probably because of the tight economic situation after the collapse of the 1826 boom. The vacant land changed hands again in 1837 at a 20 per cent premium and in 1839 four houses 'lately built' were mortgaged. These were almost certainly numbers 3, 5, 7 and 9 and were erected by James Taylor, machine maker, who had built the corner house, number 1, for himself. The conveyance of 1837 had stipulated uniform minimum conditions for the type of house to be built: at least two storeys high, fronted with best stock bricks, and roofed with Westmorland or Welsh Blue slates. The force of the covenant is clearly seen in the present appearance of the surviving numbers 7 and 9, plain and much more modest than the two Lyddon Houses. Taylor himself had no resident servants in 1841; at number 3 John Patrick, woollen manufacturer, had one; Joseph Thackray, wool merchant, had one at number 7; John Preston, solicitor, one at number 1; but Isaac Parker, warehouseman, had no servant resident at number 5.

The ground on the other side of numbers 11 and 13 was also sold by the Lyddons, and then re-sold in 1837 without having been built upon. The six houses, numbers 15 to 25, all recorded in the census of 1841 and probably dating from 1839, have identical designs which continue the alternate punctuation of doorway and window characteristic of numbers 1 to 9 with a string course between the two storeys; number 21 was taken up a further storey but its other details match its neighbours. A striking feature of the group is the six high-stepped front doors, presumably the result of raising the basement ceiling high enough to light the basement by a full-sized window, the upper half above pavement level, a feature repeated in later houses further up the road. Since none of these houses have attics it is possible that the servants slept as well as worked below stairs.

At a different point in the social scale from those who had resident servants were those who had to augment their income by taking in lodgers, and number 21 shows this distinction. Indeed number 21 also shows the fallibility of official statistics since the local enumerator entered the Aitchison household twice, twenty-six pages apart in his book, so that the checking clerks in the Registrar General's office did not notice the double entry and thus inflated the officially recorded population of Great Britain by five. The five were George Aitchison, assistant overseer of the poor for the borough; his wife; two nieces and an elderly clerk with a different surname who was probably a lodger. By the census of 1851 one niece and the clerk were no longer present, but two brothers aged 21 and 28 were specifically described as 'lodgers'. They were from Dumfries and were working as architects in Leeds. The younger, George Reid Corson, was to have a considerable impact on the architecture of Leeds, giving us the Sun Insurance building, the Municipal Buildings, the Grand Theatre, and Spenfield at Far Headingley. If Leeds went in for commemorative plaques in the GLC fashion number 21 would have more on its wall than 'Law no 1 Annexe'.

Four years after the 1841 census a public auction sale attempted to dispose of ten plots to complete the left-hand side of the Terrace and to find purchasers for fifteen plots on the right-hand side. In fact, expectations again outran reality and no houses were built on the right-hand side before 1870, and by 1851 only five of the ten plots on the left-hand side were taken. The first two of these were immediately sold to a cloth manufacturer and a wool merchant respectively, who built numbers 27 and 29. These houses mark the return to three-storey elevations and, although the heavy stonework of the doorways and windows shows that time had passed and tastes changed since numbers 21 to 25 were built, the change is less marked since the shape of the doorways is still classical. This pair of houses subsequently had their front doors blocked and new entrances made on the Clarendon Road side. Until 1884 the adjacent plots were unbuilt upon and served as gardens for number 29. Beyond the gardens numbers 37, 39 and 41 were completed between 1849 and 1851. This trio had the high-stepped front doors and large basements of earlier houses in the Terrace and abandoned the heavy stone doorways of numbers 27 and 29 for the old tradition of white classical frames. After the demolition of numbers 43 and 45 (built in 1905/06) this group has been cleaned and restored for use as student housing.

When the remaining gap was filled between 1884 and 1886 with numbers 31 to 35 the use of brick showed some conformity with the older part of the Terrace; but there is nothing classical about the carved stone lintels of numbers 33 and 35 where dormers also appear for the first time, surmounted by what look like, but cannot be, individual lightning conductors in some protophallic form. Number 31 shows the taste for heavy stone spreading beyond doorways to windows, and its iron railings depart from the plain vertical spikes of the earlier houses. It oddest feature is the overhang of the roof and gutter as if the architect

'EVERY MAN FOR HIMSELF'? THE VARIETY OF ARCHITECTURAL STYLES OF THE HOUSES ON THE EAST (RIGHT HAND) SIDE OF LYDDON TERRACE. NOS 34-40 (LEFT – NOW PART OF ELLERSLIE HALL) WERE BEGUN IN 1870 AND THE TERRACE COMPLETED (NOS. 28-20) IN 1881.

was erecting a Swiss chalet in the expectation that the Ice Age was returning to Leeds.

At the time when the Terrace was commenced as an east-facing row, Kendal Lane at its rear was insignificant (*for the making of Clarendon Road see pages 87–95 below*). The Lyddon Terrace coach-houses and outbuildings on that side have been poised for some time between dereliction and demolition; but there are welcome signs that some order is now being imposed to improve the University's image for passers-by on this busy road. It would be nice to see the oldest coach-house, in the garden of number 11, retained for some such use as a student bicycle shed.

No interest had been shown at the auction sales in any of the plots on the right-hand side of the Terrace until 1870 when numbers 30 to 34 and 2 Lifton Place (now merged into Ellerslie Hall) were commenced. Numbers 2 to 12, at the other end of the Terrace but also of the 'seventies, have been demolished. Numbers 14 and 16 were never built. Development at this southern end was not possible until after the death in 1872 of Robert Frost, tenant of number 11 at the time of the 1845 sale. As we have seen, he had gone to the 1845 sale not only to bid for number 11 but for two empty plots on the opposite side of the road to assure his view, and the purchaser of number 13 had done the same. The array of surviving houses that make up this side of the Terrace must all be dated between 1870 and 1881 but the variety of styles, sometimes within the façade of a single house, is much greater than in the whole fifty years of building represented on the other side of the Terrace. It was now every man for himself:

for example, the architect of number 28 employed a stone string course such as had unified the Terrace houses of the 'twenties and 'thirties but he did not put it at the same level as that in numbers 22 and 24; theirs was at a different level from number 26, while number 20 favoured an imitation string course in deep purple bricks. All these houses followed the distinctive Lyddon Terrace fashion of tall basements, raised ground floors and high front steps, number 28 having basement windows so high that they almost make a ground floor, while the front steps of number 20 (Law) are so steep that they actually form a bridge over a dry moat; a second flight at the south side of this building, probably once a separate house, is also a bridge with thee cast-iron pillars to support it, medieval columns with decorated capitals.

Number 28 (1879/80), like the 30 to 34 trio, favoured a Dutch treatment of its skyline. In all four the smoke-blackened stone may seem oppressive; but the benefaction which allowed the adjoining Law Faculty houses to be cleaned shows how differently the colour of the local stone appeared to the architects and first occupants.

Numbers 30 to 34 are at once Dutch in their roof line and Norman in their windows. Number 28 is Dutch in its roof line but medieval-floral in the decoration of its keystones and capitals. Number 26 is the only house to attempt a balcony: the period is clearly Renaissance, perhaps for some very slender Juliet with a convenient drainpipe for Romeo. Numbers 22 and 24 were built as a pair (1878/81) using intermixed stone and brick for their decoration and copying the door of 26 (also 1878/81) but not the balcony.

Number 20, with three Greek temples in its façade and red, white and blue brickwork above, is the unchallenged eyecatcher of the Terrace although my own preference is for the less strident dignity of numbers 11 and 13 on the other side. Number 20 was built between 1878 and 1881 for a railway contractor, James Thomson; and the oral tradition among the Law teachers is that he designed it himself but with the declining fortunes of railway contracting had to shorten his purse with a consequent descent in lavishness as one ascends. Certainly the steps to the front door climb like a railway footbridge, and underneath them is a second entrance, its stained glass door giving direct entrance to the basement. A tradesmen's entrance? A servants' basement with stained glass in all its windows as well as its door? A parquet floor within! Since there is still a plain door for tradesmen in the back street, might we have a subterranean billiard room where Mr Thomson could relax from the problems of viaducts in the Balkans and tunnels in the Andes?

The circuit of houses on the former Lyddon estate is now complete, although one other vestige of the street townscape is preserved in the campus landscape of the present day – as scattered but as welcome as its surviving trees. The stone setts that ante-date macadamised road surfaces were tough enough to resist the coaches, carts and wagons that serviced the houses and workshops of the area. In deference to the motor car there has been a tendency to smother the setts in tar, but they will be preserved for the pedestrians whose suspension is less sensitive than that of motor cars. 'Just like Beacon Hill,' said an admiring visitor from Boston, Massachusetts, recently, spotting a few yards of setts on the campus: but we cannot prove that our Lyddons spoke only to Woolcocks and the Woolcocks spoke only to God.

THE 'RAILWAY FOOTBRIDGE' TO NO 20 LYDDON TERRACE

The walk to Lyddon Terrace commences at the 'vast baronial' pair of semi-detached houses 'Roseneath' and 'The Abnalls' now identified as 5 and 7 Cromer Terrace and occupied by the Careers Service. Roseneath (No. 5) was once the home of Joseph Hepworth, the clothing pioneer (whose chain of shops were always regarded as slightly more up-market than Burton's). The house retains its glass-canopied entrance and has a charming architectural conceit – look up and you will see windows placed *within* the chimney-stacks.

The area surrounding these houses has been vastly transformed. Immediately to the west is the newly-built 'Bright Beginnings' childcare centre (architects: The Harrogate Design Group) which has replaced the former day nursery. To the south towards Lyddon Hall and Chancellor's Court, are a group of recently-built student accommodation blocks (Storm Jameson Court) (architects: Sheppard, Robson & Morgan and Ashurst Design & Build) which have replaced Mary Ogilvie House of Charles Morris Hall. These blocks step down in height with the rising land: from seven storeys adjacent to the two remaining 'tower' blocks of Charles Morris Hall to four storeys close to Roseneath and the Abnalls. Much as we may regret the demolition of Ogilvie House (designed by Christoph Bon) there is no doubt that the landscaping and layout of the new buildings is a great improvement over the previous awkward and inconveniently planned access routes.

So we begin our walk westwards towards Lyddon Terrace along the path and roadway which follows the line of the former Cloberry Street, a particularly nice feature of which is the re-introduction of stone setts in place of tarmac. We pass, on the left, the landscaped entrance to 'Bright Beginnings' and thence go past the car park and derelict Day Nursery, as visually unattractive as it was in Beresford's day.

The 'majestic pair' of houses (Nos. 11 and 13 Lyddon Terrace) were designed by J. S. Morrish, who practised in Bath before removing to Leeds in 1821 to become Mrs Lyddon's architect and agent – and it is these houses which represent the Georgian building tradition of Bath most completely. We can only regret that Morrish was unable to complete the whole of the left-hand (west) side of the terrace to the same high architectural standard. However, since Beresford wrote, the environment of Lyddon Terrace has been much improved: gone are the *Home and Gardens* door lamp at No. 11, the rainbow letter-box at No. 15 and the facing-bricks at No. 13 have been partially restored. But most significant, here as elsewhere on the campus, has been the removal of tarmac and the restoration of stone setts in the roadway. An admiring visitor from the USA may now say it is even 'more like Beacon Hill'!

There is no plaque at No. 21 to record that this was the lodging-residence of the young George Corson – but surely No. 31 is a house designed by him? Beresford likens it to a Swiss chalet, but is has more a touch of heavy Scottish Baronial – very similar in style to his warehouse in Little Germany in Bradford (46 Peckover Street), built for a Scottish company. Nos. 33 and 35 are altogether different; the decorative brickwork around the doors, windows and dormers are clear echoes of the 'Queen Anne' style.

The contrast between the blackened stone (of Nos. 34 to 28) at the northern end of Lyddon Terrace and the cleaned stone (of Nos. 26 to 20) remains to this day. One hopes that in a future restoration the former group will once again appear as they did to their first middle-class occupants.

No. 20 (Faculty of Law) with, as Beresford describes, its three Greek temples (actually pedimented door and windows) is the eye-catcher in the Terrace. I recall Beresford, declaiming to an assembled group, its history and architecture from the steps – but always keeping the lawyers on his right side! The lower servants' entrance below the steps is now bricked up, but the stained glass windows remain. These however are clearly Art Nouveau in style and are obviously much later than the building itself. The second flight of steps and bridge with cast-iron pillars has been demolished to make way for the rear extension for the Faculty of Law – not a bad job since it maintains the view along the back gardens and beyond to Lifton Place.

The car park and day nursery at the south end of Lyddon Terrace mark the frontier between the Lyddon estate and a series of street developments within the grounds of late eighteenth-century villas lying in Little Woodhouse.

THE CAPITULATION TO the spirit of development exhibited in these streets began in Springfield Place as early as 1831, that is fourteen years before Hillary Place was laid out in the grounds of Hebblethwaite's villa on Woodhouse Lane (*page 2 above*). It is a pity that Springfield Place has been demolished, for it was the first street in the modern sense to invade Woodhouse: every one of the earlier developments – such as Blenheim Terrace, Eldon Terrace, and Preston Place – was intended to be a single-sided street with all the houses having a clear southward view. Springfield Place on the other hand was designed from the first not only to have smaller houses but to have them facing similar houses across the width of the street as if in a mirror.

Springfield Place was developed by a Quaker stuff merchant, Newman Cash, who came from Coventry to buy Springfield Lodge in 1826. Springfield Lodge, later swallowed by the Women's Hospital, had been built in 1783 and was one of a series of detached villas discussed as a group below (*page 70*). The success of Springfield Place, completed in 1839, encouraged Cash to acquire more land to the north-west on the edge of the Lyddon estate, then like the sleeping princess still in Chancery and awaiting the kiss of her prince. In this field he designed Springfield Mount, a street in all but name, and with houses on both sides – but a mixture of terraces and villas rather than the continuous small terrace houses of Springfield Place. The price paid for this ambition was a much slower rate of progress, and it was 1890 before the last plot in Springfield Mount was taken up.

The original buildings of Springfield Mount are intact apart from the villas at numbers 21 and 23 which were replaced by the Hostel of the Resurrection in 1908. The sporadic development on both sides has prevented the houses having a neat chronological order, but the older houses are at the upper end and this can be reached on foot from Lyddon Terrace by crossing the car park to the rear of Woodsley Terrace and entering Springfield Mount by the footpath below Woodsley Terrace (a later development of 1856/61). There is no access to Springfield Mount from Clarendon Road.

A sale plan of 1839, when Clarendon Road was itself being initiated, shows numbers 25 and 27 Springfield Mount already completed. These two villas have been extended and then amalgamated, first for the Mount Hotel and now for the Mount Medical Residences. Their original architecture is thus obscured but the next oldest villa, number 19, is unaltered and an interesting example of a single façade concealing two houses within, rather like a superior back-to-back house. It is now owned by the Health Authority and divided into four flats with a new side entrance. The former front door is in use but the street gates are blocked; the former back entrance and the stables are now reached from Hyde Terrace. The villa was built between 1837 and 1839 – just in time to qualify as Victorian. Its remarkable features are the pairs of pilasters applied to each wall to frame the doors; four more appear as pure decoration on the south face. Like pilasters on Anglo-Saxon churches they are not functional. Unlike their stylistic cousins on the terraces of Bath and Cheltenham they refuse to be Greek, although

19 SPRINGFIELD MOUNT 'ANGLO-EGYPTIAN OF 1837-39'.

fluted. Is not the square incised pattern Anglo-Egyptian like Marshall's flax mill in Holbeck (1838/40)? – although it was in woollens and not linen that its first co-owners, Joseph Burras and William Binns, clothdressers, were occupied.

The original census enumerators' returns, completed for the night of 7/8 June 1841, support the suggestion of an original division, for under 'Bethel House, Springfield Crescent' were recorded William Binns, clothdresser, his wife, two brothers, four children, and three ladies with independent means, perhaps lodgers. There were no servants, which certainly suggests that things were a little pinched, for (as we shall see) even smaller houses in the street had at least one servant. The next entry, 'Springfield Crescent', was for Joseph Burras, Binns' business partner, also a clothdresser, his wife, mother, four children, and a sister who was acting as family servant (a further hint of straitened circumstances – 1841 was a year of considerable commercial distress and textile unemployment). The 'Crescent' was a curious name for half a building that was quite four-square but there was vacant ground between it and the present Faversham Hotel until number 17 was commenced in 1877: the two partners may therefore have intended to create a small crescent but been checked by economic difficulties.

The census enumerators' returns may be used for other purposes than confirming the date of a building: the information about occupants is detailed enough to throw light on the social and economic position of those for whom the houses were built and of the successive occupants. There are difficulties in Springfield Mount, however, since the villas were not assigned numbers in the 1841 census and the houses were renumbered more than once as gaps between villas were closed by later buildings. It is likely however that the census entry for William Stow, 'merchant', with a wife, four children, six female servants, and one male servant, relates to number 27 (The Mount). It is significant that no other house in the district except Fairbairn's (i.e. Woodsley House *page 92 below*) aspired to male servants in 1841.

Number 2, Hillel House, was not yet built in 1841: so we cannot match its lavish exterior to a domestic interior until the census of 1851, when R. J. Ellershaw, oil merchant and soap maker, lived there with his wife, a younger unmarried sister, four children, a cook, a housemaid, and two nurses. By 1851 William Stow had left number 27 but it was still well-staffed: R. L. Ford, the solicitor, had a governess and four female servants in residence to cater for himself, his wife and six children. Burras and Binns had then left number 19 and half the villa was uninhabited. The two families who inhabited the large divided villa built *c.*1850 that has now been transformed into the Faversham Hotel had three servants each, and there was a family in the cosy little octagonal lodge that stands alongside the University security shelter where the same daily duty is performed – the recognition of unwanted callers, for the Mount was intended as a private road with no thoroughfare for vehicles into Clarendon Road which had not then been developed.

The protracted development has intermingled architectural periods, and it is time to resume a more orderly progress in these *Walks*, beginning at the original entrance by the little lodge. From this approach the view is dominated by Hillel House (number 2), built in 1845 for a tea merchant and constructed in the conventional Leeds style of postponed Georgian using red brick with stone

SPRINGFIELD MOUNT — A COSY OCTAGONAL LODGE OF *c*.1850.

quoins. The date of the male cherubs who hold a scallop aloft on an oval window and of the trunkless cherub on another window is unknown. Like the nakedness of the cherubs, the red brick has been prudishly covered – but only recently – with a colour wash which emphasises the quoins' black paint, the decorator obviously thinking he had a contract for a Cumbrian manor house.

The fate of number 4 is no better. The Mount Preston side has been given the front door; and the Springfield Mount façade with its lovely sixteen-pane windows now has a fine display of lavatory plumbing. Is it for students with bowel complaints, one wonders, sympathetically.

This side of Springfield Mount was conceived as a terrace, with smaller plots offered for sale than for the villas on the south side. By 1841 the development had commenced but not on adjoining plots. The brickwork shows that numbers 6 and 8 were built together. In 1841 they were occupied by a linen manufacturer and a woollen manufacturer respectively (four and three servants in residence). But number 10 was not built until 1867; number 10A not until 1885, a very late insert as its style and number indicate. Number 12 missed the 1841 census by three years. In 1841 numbers 14 and 16 were part of the first development stage, with the flax dresser John Armistead (two servants) at number 14, and at number 16 George Morton (one servant), wallpaper manufacturer with premises at 3 Commercial Street. George Morton is a key figure in the development of Springfield Mount and the students who live in the University flats there should perhaps take him as their patron saint, for it was he who built for resale numbers

32 SPRINGFIELD MOUNT.

HILLEL HOUSE (2 SPRINGFIELD MOUNT).

THE GATEWAY TO THE PRIORY OF ST WILFRED IN SPRINGFIELD MOUNT.

6/8 and 14/16, as well as 22/24/26, although only number 22 of that trio was actually erected by census night, with the family and three servants of a gentleman of independent means in residence. Numbers 24 and 26 were probably occupied by 1844, the former by an oil merchant with twenty-four persons in employment at his works and three servants living in his house; his neighbour, a clerk in a newspaper office, had a wife but no children and yet also had two servants.

The terrace was not completed until numbers 18 and 20 were erected to fill the gap in 1864/66. The detached pair of houses that make numbers 28 and 30 were actually caught 'in building' on census night 1861 although there was a mysterious earlier development of servants' quarters and workshops at the back of this plot on Mount Preston which can still be seen. Number 32, the solid detached villa next to Woodsley Terrace, was occupied on that census night by Edward Walker, 'railway shareholder', with his wife, daughter, two nieces, and two servants. Since 1845 Walker had been living with his father, a 'landed proprietor', at number 25 opposite. The large plot of land between number 32 and Clarendon Road remained empty until 1856 when the eight houses of Woodsley Terrace were commenced, being completed by the census of 1861.

On the opposite side of the road, the six houses that make up numbers 7 to 17 (originally named The Esplanade) were on the land where Burras had intended the Crescent in 1840. Fortune did not smile on the development, even when number 13 was renumbered. The architect, John Hall, seems to have joined Burras' son in the development, and in 1877 building started with number 17 (the present Obstetrics Department with its original front door wide enough to admit pregnant triplets side by side). It was 1890 before number 7 received its first occupant, Mr Schuddekopf, Professor of Languages.

Now to three invisible houses and two transformations. There never was a number 5; and numbers 21 and 23 are invisible because they were demolished in 1908 for the building of the Priory of St Wilfrid (the Hostel of the Resurrection). This important building was erected in Leeds by the Community of the Resurrection to enable candidates economically debarred from Oxbridge to enter the Anglican priesthood by reading for degrees in theology at Leeds University. This project to rescue future Judes the Obscure was housed in a red brick medieval-cum-Tudor building modelled on an Oxbridge college with an interior quadrangle, and its gate-house incorporated in what Pevsner has described as 'a noble façade'. The chapel on the first floor to the right of the gate-house has been converted to a lecture theatre, and the refectory on the left to a common room. The quasimonastic cell bedrooms now provide rooms for lecturers and clerical staff of the University Adult Education Centre, a transformation which would have been not unacceptable to Hardy's Jude.

The lesser second transformation had taken place at number 22 opposite. Anyone looking at the front of number 22 could rightly ask whether I have taken leave of my senses to include it in George Morton's development of 1840, for it has every flourish of the mid-Victorian, and it is identical with numbers 18 and 20 that have been already assigned to 1864/66. But conveyances cannot lie – especially those in the West Riding Registry of Deeds at Wakefield which record Morton's sale to Thomas Walker; moreover the house is on a plan of 1844 and

THE PRIORY OF ST WILFRED IN SPRINGFIELD MOUNT.

the Ordnance map of 1850. What transformation, then? A walk to the back of the house gives the clue, for from there it can be seen at once that the backside of number 22 fails in every particular to match numbers 18 and 20. When the latter were built, the opportunity must have been taken to remodel the façade of number 22 to match them without altering the back. An inspection of the interior may confirm: but please ring the bell.

The Mount Hotel and Mount Medical Residences have been wholly rebuilt by the Leeds Partnerships NHS Foundation Trust and there is no access from Springfield Mount. The condition of the houses and general environment of Springfield Mount are much the same as when Beresford wrote – from the well-manicured lawn and cream-painted façade of Hillel Student Centre to the unkempt and debris-strewn front gardens at the upper end of the Mount. The Esplanade (Nos. 7 to 17) is now wholly occupied by student flats. The mid-Victorian flourish which Beresford describes in Nos. 18, 20 and 22 is clearly expressed in the doorways, set between Corinthian columns and surmounted by bold architraves.

The Hostel of the Resurrection, or the Priory of St Wilfred, is indeed the noblest building in Springfield Mount – and arguably the noblest building in the whole University campus. Yet for many people, staff and students alike, its very existence is unknown. It was designed by one of the greatest late Victorian architects, Temple Moore, in 1907-10, with extensions by his son, Leslie Moore in 1927-28. The Adult Education Centre is now a thing of the past and the building has been converted, with a degree of sensitivity, to residential accommodation. Please ring the bell if you wish to see the wonderful interior.

This Walk is a mere link from Springfield Mount to Little Woodhouse Hall, but it merits a separate chapter because of the historic importance of Springfield House and its role in subverting the proposed extension to the Chamberlin Plan.

THE CARRIAGE WAY from which the backs of Springfield Mount have just been inspected was laid out to give access to the coach-houses of the larger houses, some of which eventually became small workshops before reverting to their original use as garages. It also served the rear of the demolished Mount Preston, a street now submerged under the lawns of Charles Morris Hall.

At the lower end of Mount Preston, near the Senior Common Room, was the frontier between the Lyddon estate (hence 'Preston'), the Springfield Lodge estate of Newman Cash, and a third estate of smaller size and rather different development. It originated in June 1792 when the clothdresser Thomas Livesey bought a field with the name Well Close, a name perhaps linked to the 'spring' of the neighbouring Springfield Lodge which was then nine years old. In Well Close Livesey built Springfield House in the same style as Claremont, the demolished Belmont and the now revitalised Belle Vue (*page 84 below*). It now stands in a car park behind the octagonal lodge at the foot of Springfield Mount, facing the Worsley Medical and Dental Building across Clarendon Way.

When originally built it had workshops and warehouses adjoining like its contemporaries the Rhodes house at Beech Grove and Wainhouse's Belle Vue. These, together with the coach houses, greenhouses, garden sheds, and outbuildings, have been demolished. In this truncated form it is now a Listed Building but it has not been well treated in the immediate past, either internally or externally, and its intended development as a Student Health Centre has been frustrated by cuts in public spending. Barricaded windows and padlocked doors try to close their eyes to the fact that for the foreseeable future the only callers will be cars coming to park in the former garden at the front and the University gardeners bringing decaying leaves to the compost heaps at the rear. Boys of some size or other have painted football posts on one side, and at the front a University notice solemnly warns passers-by that the 'Building is Dangerous'. Others will recognise it as the back-drop for al fresco drinking under the Faversham mulberry tree.

The terms of an advertisement in the *Leeds Mercury* of 17 May 1799 match the particulars in a fire insurance policy of 1805 for £2000 and indicate a mixture of domestic and commercial premises not uncommon at the new houses of Leeds merchants, whether in Little Woodhouse or along the Harrogate turnpike.

To judge from the wording of the advertisement, it was clearly not detrimental to social status if cloth dried on the tenter frames in the next field or if smoke arose from a dye-house at the foot of the garden. Common rights on the Moor (since extinguished) were useful for pack-horses and coach-horses. A private road, a wagon's width, ran down to Park Lane and the town centre past Little Woodhouse Hall (*page 79*).

Newspaper advertisements failed to sell Springfield House in 1799, and in 1803 it was offered to let. In 1813 Thomas Livesey was bankrupted and until 1833 the estate was sterilised for any development by bankruptcy proceedings.

SPRINGFIELD HOUSE – AS IT WAS IN 1982 (PHOTOGRAPH COURTESY OF ENGLISH HERITAGE).

SPRINGFIELD HOUSE AS IT IS NOW – A NEW LEASE OF LIFE.

It then had the misfortune of further inaction whilst a Chancery suit was fought for three years. The court authorised a sale in 1836 when the house and most of the grounds were purchased by the sitting tenant, Samuel Birchall, a Quaker woolstapler. Despite the development potential mentioned in the 1799 advertisement, Birchall left his estate sylvan and increased it by arranging to take up a field on the western flank from the area that the Atkinsons were then trying to develop as Hyde Terrace (*page 97 below*). He lived in Springfield House until his death in 1854, and when his family put the estate up for sale in 1865 the property was bought by the Roman Catholic diocese and a large seminary erected alongside the old house which then became the diocesan office; no street building occurred in its grounds until three short rows of back-to-backs were built near Little Woodhouse Street in 1891, the Mentones, now demolished.

Springfield House played a pivotal role in the abandonment of the Chamberlin Development Plan. Despite the upward-revised estimates of student numbers following the publication of the Robbins Report in 1963, no further revision of the plan was made. At the same time there was an increasing disillusion with 'modern' architecture – a disillusion which found concrete expression in the collapse of the Ronan Point Flats in 1968 – and a corresponding growing strength of the conservation movement. The crisis came in 1971. Springfield House and the seminary stood in the way of Chamberlin's proposed biological sciences building and extensions to the hospital buildings. The seminary was demolished *c.*1975 but happily Springfield House was listed as a building of architectural and historic interest.

The University applied for Listed Building Consent for its demolition which was refused. The case went to appeal and in 1975 Listed Building Consent for demolition was again refused. It was a severe blow to Chamberlin who was unable to accept either the inspector's ruling or the necessity of amending the Development Plan in accordance with conservation restraints. In 1978 Peter Chamberlin died and the University's contract with the firm of Chamberlin, Powell and Bon was terminated.

Springfield House, which now houses the Covance Development Services Company, has now been restored (although little of the interior remained), on each side wings have been built, angled slightly forward, and what is in effect a garden has been created along the frontage. The whole now forms a very pleasant enclave approached via the octagonal lodge which is easily overlooked.

From the garden at the front of Springfield House the (now mature) planting of silver-birch trees and the hedge hide (except in winter) what must be the most horrible building on the Leeds campus – the Worsley Medical and Dental building not designed by Chamberlin, Powell and Bon but by the Building Design Partnership. Its oppressive bulk, the narrow windows squeezed in between vertical strips of grey concrete slabs, remind one of the 'Ministry of Love' in George Orwell's novel *1984*. One might almost imagine the same black-uniformed guards roaming round its perimeter, armed with rubber truncheons. As it is the only warning notices are those about 'no smoking' in hospital grounds.

Continuing on the footpath to the west of Springfield House we descend to Hyde Terrace and continue along Hyde Street to Clarendon Road. On our left we follow a red brick wall which turns left again into Little Woodhouse Street, from which vantage-point we have the best view, over the wall, of Little Woodhouse Hall.

THIS HOUSE IS probably the oldest in the district. It stood on Kendal Lane facing the cottages of the hamlet across a small green which survived until about 1960. A sketch of its façade *c.*1740 has been preserved among a solicitor's papers in the Leeds City Archives Department, and in 1742 a more direct access to Leeds than the twisting Kendal Lane was achieved by purchasing a narrow strip of land for a carriage way down to Park Lane, the present narrow Chorley Lane between Clarendon Road and Belmont Grove. The older part of the house is the west wing; the house was enlarged by later owners in 1821 and 1830 and the main entrance moved to the side, where its gates now face the Dental Hospital.

On the wall at the rear a long-obsolete notice proclaims 'City of Leeds: Child Guidance Clinic'. The building had been badly vandalised by children beyond all guidance, and one hopes that the Hospital Authority, its present owners, will be able to revivify it, although it has become through delay and neglect a gaunt cripple of a house having the air of a patient with a terminal illness who knows his fate better than the surgeons who console him. This is the house where the young Millais was commissioned to decorate; later the city's Judges' Lodgings when Leeds became an assize town; and more recently part of the College of Art. Occupation alone will breathe life into it; the ugly but necessary barriers to vandals, not fully effective, obscure an appreciation of its fine staircases and generous rooms.

THE EAST WING (FACING THE DENTAL INSTITUTE) OF LITTLE WOODHOUSE HALL (*c.*1830)
WITH A DORIC PORCH ADDED BY JOHN CLARK *c.*1840.

(It is pleasing to know that one's hopes for old buildings are sometimes met:
since these words were initially written, the Hospital Authority has started upon
the major task of re-roofing the Hall preparatory to converting it to Hospital
staff residences, with the result that the invalid now has a life support system
in the form of scaffolding and its own team of – rather brawny – doctors
and nurses.)

In the *c.*1740 sketch, the building is described as 'The Manor House at Little Woodhouse'. Freda
Matthews tells me that it was very probably Maurice Beresford himself, and Dorothy Payne, the
historian of Claremont, who first called it 'Little Woodhouse Hall'. However, Beresford's hopes have
been fully realised. Little Woodhouse Hall has now been superbly restored as a residential home
by the Leeds Community Healthcare Trust and the red brick of the south-facing façade (seen over
the cement-rendered stone wall of Little Woodhouse Street which follows the former alignment of
Kendal Lane) gleams as never before. The rear (north) elevations are covered in bright yellow stucco
and are linked to sympathetically-scaled new buildings in red brick. One curiosity concerns the
entrances in the East Wing facing the Dental Institute which consist of two, not one, pairs of
massive gateposts in red brick with gritstone quoins and separated by a short length of brick wall.
These presumably date from the time when the Hall was divided into two separate dwellings listed
as 18 Clarendon Road and 2 Hyde Terrace. Indeed, in the car park to the rear of the hall there are
the remains of a boundary wall which separated the two gardens.

Although this Walk takes us well beyond the University campus, it allows us to better appreciate how the campus relates to the earlier pattern of development in this part of Leeds. We encounter fragments of a pre-turnpike lane and later eighteenth-century building schemes which were as grandiose in their day as the University building schemes of the twentieth century.

ALTHOUGH THE UNIVERSITY properties do not extend over the whole of Little Woodhouse, the development of Hyde Terrace and Clarendon Road is only explicable as the culmination of earlier and frustrated attempts to develop the fields further south and west between the manor house and Park Lane,

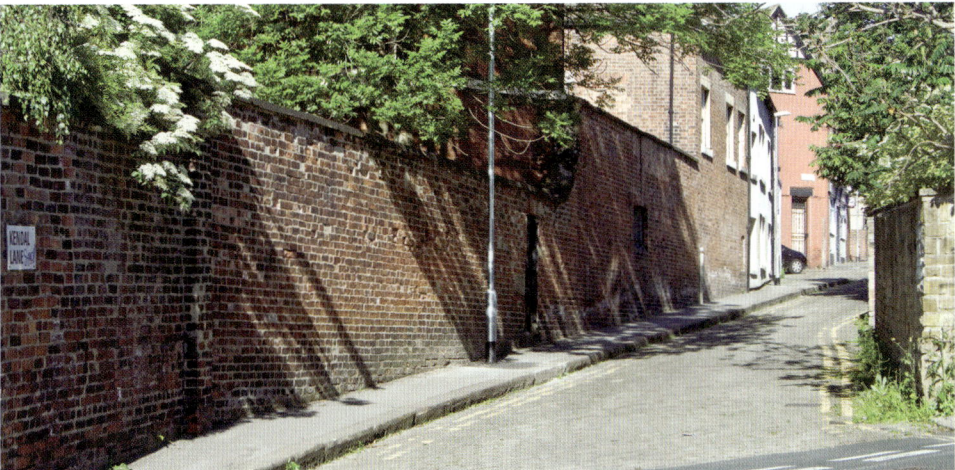

KENDAL LANE – THE PRE-TURNPIKE ROAD FROM LEEDS TO THE MOOR AT ITS JUNCTION WITH CLARENDON ROAD.

necessitating a short detour outside the campus although with the bonus of a sight of some important red brick architecture.

The first stage of development in the fields of Little Woodhouse followed a familiar course, the erection of a detached gentleman's residence. But in this area we encounter in two squares a form of street development new to these *Walks*; although behind Woodhouse Lane two similar developments south of the University can be visited at Queen Square (1806) and Blenheim Square (1831). The Little Woodhouse Squares and the Woodhouse Lane Squares also exhibit, through their range of architectural styles, the result of abortive schemes and failed speculation similar to those encountered elsewhere on the campus.

Through the fields of Little Woodhouse, just above the riverside meadows, ran anciently two roads: one, surviving as Kendal Lane, climbed the hill towards Great Woodhouse Moor, thence to Otley, Skipton and Kendal; the other ran due west along the contour towards Burley and Kirkstall Bridge. By the 1790s Park Lane and this western continuation into Burley Road marked not only the principal road from Leeds to Kirkstall and Bradford but the southern boundary for a series of seven gentlemen's estates based on a line of houses set along Kendal Lane as it climbed the ridge to the north, giving each a view down to the Aire over the garden and carriage drive. Little Woodhouse Hall was the earliest of these (*c.*1740) and the other three survivors can be reached by following the narrow Kendal Lane westwards from its crossing with Clarendon Road opposite the Hall. Three others of the seven – Mount Preston (*c.*1780), Springfield Lodge (1783) and Belmont (1786) – have already fallen to the demolition contractors in the cause of hospital and medical school building.

Claremont, where there has been a house since at least 1742, stands opposite Little Woodhouse Hall, separated now by Clarendon Road but originally only

DENISON HALL (1786); THE LARGEST HOUSE OF ITS DAY IN LEEDS.

by a brick wall. Its back gate gave on to Kendal Lane, and it had a two-storey wing of counting house and workshops, part of which, cut into by the later creation of Claremont Avenue, is now used for overseas students flatlets. In this house lived Dr J. D. Heaton, chairman of the appeal committee that launched the Yorkshire College of Science and hence godfather of the University. On his death there was no possibility of making a square from the gardens of Claremont since part had already been absorbed at the making of Woodhouse Square. Instead the ground was developed from 1896, first with the line of Claremont Villas facing Clarendon Road, a new street, Claremont Avenue (where these words were initially typed), and then the cul-de-sac Claremont Grove, all complete by 1898. The safety of Claremont from demolition had been ensured by institutional use as the home of the Thoresby Society, the Yorkshire Archaeological Society and the Leeds Civic Trust.

Behind the houses in Claremont Grove are remains of a high brick wall which once separated Claremont from the grounds of its grander neighbour, Denison Hall, which also turned its back on Kendal Lane in order to achieve a sunny south face for the principal rooms. Denison Hall, sometimes called Woodhouse Park to differentiate it from Little Woodhouse Hall, was built for John Denison in 1786. Dr R. G. Wilson put the monument to John Denison on the jacket of his book *Gentlemen Merchants*: but it is significant that the monument stands not in a Leeds church but in one at Ossington, Nottinghamshire, near the country house for which Denison abandoned his new Leeds home only a few years after building it. After his departure the Hall was divided vertically to make two rented mansions but was later bought for the potential value of the building ground surrounding it. It has been restored to a unity in its present use as an old people's hostel.

Magnificent as its southern front still is – the largest house in the borough until Roundhay Hall was built in 1826 – its true character as the home of a Gentleman Merchant is obscured by the demolition of the stables, wagon shed, counting house, and cloth finishing shops that fire insurance policies record in the 1790s. New houses cover their traces but their high walls still abut on to Kendal Lane.

In the 1820s it was hoped to utilise the extensive grounds to the south of Denison Hall to lay out a square in the Bath or Bloomsbury fashion, to be loyally christened Hanover Square. This failed as the business boom collapsed and a second venture, floated in 1840, was as partial in its achievement as Woodhouse Square. Hanover Square had its private road leading up from Park Lane, Hanover Street, with a porter's lodge and gate to ensure privacy. The lodge was removed when Park Lane College was built but three of the Square's original houses survive in the south-western corner and their owners seem to be bringing colour back into once invalid cheeks. The enormous house in the middle of the east side was once owned by Edward Baines Jr, MP and proprietor-editor of the Whig trumpet, the *Leeds Mercury*. Use as a hostel has preserved it, and it is always a pleasure to see Christmas decorations swinging from ceilings whose first owner had known Charles Dickens. But the failure of the Hanover Square venture is indicated by the much later date of the houses alongside and on the other two sides of the Square.

Behind the houses on the west side of the Square is an open space where back-to-back houses have been cleared and the planners' decision awaited At the far side of this mixture of debris and grass-grown street surfaces Belle Vue stands in splendid isolation, just as it did when Michael Wainhouse built it *c*.1793. At that date there would have been truly a striking Belle Vue across the Aire valley from this commanding spot, as indeed there still is despite the invasion of industry. Wainhouse himself brought industry to the area by erecting a steam-powered mill, Little Woodhouse Mill, where his garden ran alongside Park Lane but with little loss of amenity since it was half-concealed by the abrupt fall in ground level.

Otherwise the grounds of Belle Vue remained unbuilt upon even while Belle Vue Road was being developed further along the scarp in the eighteen-sixties. Only in the 'seventies did Belle Vue acquire as closer neighbours several streets of back-to-back houses, two of these actually built against its sides. The marks of these limpets could be seen on the side of the house before the scaffolding went up for the restorative work which has now brought the building back into use as a student residence.

The most direct route back to the University campus from Belle Vue takes us through the multi-period Hanover Square and past the rear of Park Lane College to the south-west corner of Woodhouse Square across which the crags of the Worsley Medical and Dental Building can be seen proving that medical as well as social scientists can have their heads in the clouds. In Woodhouse Square lay the origin of Clarendon Road.

Claremont continues to be the home of the Thoresby Society and the Yorkshire Archaeological Society (Leeds Civic Trust now has its home in Wharf Street, just off Kirkgate in Leeds City Centre). The house was 'new built' for a Quaker Merchant, John Elam in 1772, but may be a Georgian 'wrap-around' an earlier building, as suggested by the change in structure at the rear. Certainly, a house has existed on this site since Tudor Times. The house was altered after 1856 with porch and bay windows added by George Corson (architect, *inter alia* of Leeds Grand Theatre) for Dr John Deakin Heaton. Inside may be found a fine eighteenth-century cantilevered stone staircase and some fittings from demolished houses 'rescued' by the Yorkshire Archaeological Society. The high brick wall to which Beresford refers is something of a mystery. It is certainly evident in a *c*.1870s photograph of the croquet lawn of Claremont (complete with the members of Dr Heaton's family) and probably followed the alignment of the present back Claremont Terrace. But in its continuation downhill it appears to have been built of stone – and it is the remains of this stone wall which can be glimpsed at the cul-de-sacs of Claremont View and Claremont Grove.

To access Denison Hall and Hanover Square we proceed along the ancient road, Kendal Lane (named after John Kendal, Elizabethan owner of the Little Woodhouse Estate, not the town in Cumbria) which skirts the rear of Claremont and separated from it by a high stone wall. Passing on our left Claremont Avenue (No. 4 was Beresford's home for many years) and Back Claremont Terrace we turn left into Hanover Square.

In my view Beresford severely underrates the architectural and townscape quality of Hanover Square. The vista as we approach from the narrow confines of Kendal Lane is breathtaking. It is one of the great, and remarkably little-known, set pieces of Leeds. It is true, as he describes, that the original plans were 'partial in their achievements' but the later (1870s) two-storey terraces which largely enclose the square (and which echo, in their architectural detailing those of Clarendon Place

'CLAREMONT', 23 CLARENDON ROAD AND ITS GARDEN BEFORE THE DEVELOPMENT
OF ITS GROUNDS IN 1896.

BELLE VUE AS IT WAS IN 1975 BEFORE RESTORATION, SURROUNDED BY BACK-TO-BACK HOUSES.
(COMPARE WITH SPRINGFIELD HOUSE, PAGE 76.)

in the University precinct) are by no means insignificant. Moreover, on the south side of the square there is one highly commendable development – a new-build of houses which precisely match, both in their scale and detailing, those adjacent.

Denison Hall itself, which occupies the whole of the north side of the square (and which is now converted into luxury flats), was designed by William Lindley of Doncaster, a pupil of John Carr of York, and the hand of the master can clearly be recognised in the Adamish south-facing elevation which overlooks a private garden laid out by Joshua Major and promoted as 'Hanover Square Park'. And although the associated stables are long gone (an insurance policy of 1812 makes no mention of cloth finishing shops), there is much residential new-build to the west which helps to sustain the true character of Denison Hall as the house of a 'gentleman merchant'.

The few buildings in the square which were completed according to the original plan are readily recognised. However, as a consequence of the renumbering of the houses (twice!) Beresford errs as to their occupancy. The 'enormous house in the middle of the east side' (now No. 11) was designed as two houses, built in 1826-30 for one John Clapham who planned further, unrealised, developments here. Georgian, six bays wide and three storeys high, it dominates its humbler neighbours. Edward Baines Jr lived in the block of four houses at the far south western corner of the square, clearly of the same period. His house (No. 38) and that of his neighbour George Rawson (No. 37), a partner in the development of the square, are distinguished by a remarkably bold entrance, framed by paired Tuscan columns supporting a heavy entablature.

It is from this south-western corner that we make our way to Park Lane and thence to Belle Vue Road, noticing en route the ground floor shell of the former Hanover Place Chapel (1847 by James Simpson, now ADP House, a mosque). The route from the northern end of the square, past Denison Hall, is much more difficult. In the 1970s the planners have replaced the rows of back-to-back houses which once existed west of the square by three-storey blocks of council dwellings (Kendal Close and Grove) and, south of Kendal Bank, private housing of a similar period – irregularly arranged for a picturesque effect and to avoid the rigid monotony of the earlier housing. But the practical effect is that access to Belle Vue Road is by narrow stepped and partly concealed pathways. Belle Vue still stands in splendid isolation, but the 'Belle Vue' is no longer obscured by industry but, as Peter Leach says in The Buildings of England: *Yorkshire West Riding*, the gargantuan blocks of student flats which line Burley Road and Park Lane.

The order in which houses in Clarendon Road are visited in this section of the Walks is a compromise. On completion in 1897 there were eighty-eight houses with dates from 1839 onwards and a strict chronological treatment would dart breathlessly up and down the hill. We must begin at the foot since the road was projected from Little Woodhouse Hall on fields belonging to it and complementing the incomplete project of Woodhouse Square. Yet the first and most important house was at the top of the hill, so that, once there, the itinerary will abandon chronology and sketch the development near Woodsley House and the Grammar School before returning house-by-house down the hill to Woodhouse Square.

IN 1825, WHEN Woodhouse Square was first projected, the owner of Little Woodhouse Hall was John Atkinson, partner in the town's most eminent firm of solicitors, and the square was designed to occupy part of the land which he had bought from Claremont to add to that in front of the Hall. Only two houses were erected before the scheme collapsed and nothing more was done until after Atkinson's death in 1833 except the sale of land adjoining Park Lane on which Francis Chorley's mills were built.

Together with Wainhouse's mill at Belle View their chimneys could be relied upon to bring down smoke and soot, but the advertisement for the revised project of a square in 1836 whistled bravely to keep its courage up: 'well adapted for genteel Residences having the advantages of the Town with Country Air'. This invasion of industry gave a curiously mixed character to this part of the west end of Leeds: on the one hand the mills, and on the other the new middle-class church of St George's (1836), Little Woodhouse Hall itself and, at the far end of Clarendon Road, a house fit for Queen Victoria to sleep in.

THE FORMER GRAMMAR SCHOOL (RIGHT) (NOW UNIVERSITY BUSINESS SCHOOL) AND CHAPEL
WHICH NOW HOUSES THE UNIVERSITY OF LEEDS INTERNATIONAL TEXTILE ARCHIVE.

The hesitancy of development after 1836 was visible not only in the failure
to take Woodhouse Square even the full length of its southern side but in the
interrupted progress of the two streets, Clarendon Road and Hyde Terrace, that
John Atkinson's legatees laid out in the six fields north of the Hall which they
had inherited with it.

Clarendon Road was designed to begin just to the west of the new and then
fashionable church, St George's, continuing the line of Great George Street into
the east side of Woodhouse Square. From the top of the Square it began to climb
the hill in a sweeping curve towards the corner of the Moor, rejoining Kendal
Lane which was thence to be widened and utilised for the final stretch behind
Lyddon terrace. A gate and gate-keeper's house at this point were designed to
emphasise the privacy but never built.

Woodsley House (now Fairburn House) was built on land purchased in 1839
and 1840. Its owner was Peter Fairbairn, partner in the Wellington Foundry,
engineer and machine-maker, and the Queen's host in 1858. His statue, as Sir
Peter Fairbairn, now stands at the foot of Clarendon Road, on the corner of
Woodhouse Square and within sight of John Atkinson's home. Fairbairn had
been previously living at 11 Park Square, then an area of dwindling
fashionability. His new house was designed to be a detached villa, not part of a

terrace or square such as formed the old west end of Leeds on the Park estate. It was not to be a miniature country house in a setting of lawns, like Gott's mansion at Armley, although its Greek portico façade looks to the same classical models as Gott. In taking the most commanding site in the road, just as it begins to wind downhill, Fairbairn was restricted to a quite small depth of plot by the shape of the fields that made up the Atkinson estate. Width was achieved by adding a second plot to the first but, even so, the front door is remarkably near the public highway for a house aiming at social distinction. On census night 1841 the family was out-numbered by servants, eight to four; and in 1861 there were ten resident servants, the largest number in any house of the west end of Leeds. By that date Fairbairn had succeeded in achieving a little more seclusion by purchasing land from the trustees of Harrison's charity that lay on the other side of Kendal Lane. This narrow winding lane ran near the back windows of Woodsley House; but in 1859, the year after the Queen's visit, Fairbairn applied to Quarter Sessions to divert the lane to the present Victoria Street (echoing the name of his recent guest), take its former course into the garden, and there join his old purchase to his new. The dead-end stop of Kendal Lane near Victoria Street can still be seen behind the residential block, which now occupies most of the former gardens of (now Fairburn) House.

This prestigious building was slow to attract neighbours. When private treaty sales failed to materialise and the estate was put up for auction in sixty-three lots in April 1847 there were still only two houses in the road, Fairbairn's and a very much smaller neighbour's, lower down the hill on the same side of the road and set so far back from the frontage line that even today it is easy to miss it. This was Airedale Mount, the present number 65, built for Mr William Bland, gentleman, by 1844 on a plot purchased in 1842.

Not a single plot seems to have been sold at the auction of 1847, and even in 1858, when Queen Victoria drove by, only four more plots had been taken, and these lay at the southern end of the road near Woodhouse Square.

Sir Peter Fairbairn died at Woodsley House in 1861. His son, to become Sir Andrew, lived in the house until 1870 but must have contemplated leaving as early as 1865 when he put the grounds of the house up for auction in forty-four building plots of various sizes (from 3600 to 900 square yards) with two plots on the Victoria Street side actually being cut from his father's rose gardens. The fields to the Grammar School side were to be developed firstly with a line of villas alongside 'Fairbairn Road' and then with villas on Clarendon Road and much smaller plots making up the Kelso Road development behind them, no more than 400 square yards for each house and garden.

Nothing happened in the way of villas until 1872 when Isaac and James Dodgshun, partners in a firm of woolstaplers, built Clarendon Villa, now Berkeley House. Mountfields, its neighbour, was not built until 1888/90 and 'Fairbairn Road' was never completed through to Belle Vue Road, being still a private unmetalled and unnamed road. On the Clarendon Road frontage Moorlands and Montrose House were built between 1872 and 1877 but the remainder of the frontage was not developed before 1890/92 when a terrace of six houses, numbers 83 to 93, was erected. Their uniformity and their narrow, though pleasantly long, front gardens mark them off from the architecturally varied villas with their wide frontages and the curving paths to their front doors. The first occupant of the end house next to the Grammar School was Mr E. H. Hepper, the auctioneer, who might be expected to have known a good site when he saw one. His neighbours included a book keeper, a traveller, an agent, and a railway inspector.

The acceptance of smaller buildings in the last plots to be developed is a normal feature when development was spread over half a century: as the years passed, the social tone of the road fell, partly through the availability of genteel villas in the new suburbs of Headingley, Chapel Allerton and Potter Newton, and partly through the higher density building by other developers on adjoining fields. Mount Preston and Springfield Place, as we have seen, had very small terrace houses built in the 1830s and 1840s; there were back-to-backs on Kendal Lane.

No back-to-back demeaned the vicinity of Woodsley House, but it is significant that when plot 45 of the 1865 sale plan was eventually taken up – not until 1891 – it was filled with six terrace houses, the present numbers 42 to 50 and 33 Hyde Terrace. This plot, the deeds show, had not been part of the original Fairbairn purchase of 1840 but one acquired in the year that he hosted Queen Victoria: it lay right opposite his front windows and was presumably bought for privacy.

A house as large as Woodsley House was itself something of a problem. Earlier in the century the Denisons had found difficulty in disposing of Denison Hall when they themselves became country gentlemen. 'Too large for a man of moderate fortune,' commented the *Leeds Guide* of 1806, 'and too near the town to be relished by the country gentlemen.' For a short while after 1870 a Gott rented Woodsley House, thereby retaining it in the best industrial families, but thereafter it could find only institutional owners: as a vicarage, a nursing home, the Leeds Clergy School, and then as a University hall of residence where the present writer was once interviewed by the late Professor Ruse as a prospective sub-warden – although he cannot recollect being offered Queen Victoria's bedroom.

There was a small amount of development down the hill in the 1850s and 1860s. At the upper end there was little: number 63 with its two-colour brick ornamentation may reflect the taste of the first occupant, the artist John Battye Tootal (1857/61). Nothing of the taste of the Unitarians can be discerned in its neighbour number 61, built as a manse for their minister, Thomas Hincks, in 1862, a plainer building than the two contemporary Anglican vicarages in Hyde Terrace: this house, Mountside, followed the path to institutional use as a 'House of Detention'. Opposite, number 40 (1867/70) was built as Southfield House for the dyer James Reffitt: it is in a romantic vein with a tower and great lightning conductor shaped like a giant's boot-scraper; at its front door marble appears for the first time in this road as an external building material to enliven the normal combination of Yorkshire stone and red brick.

In the lower part of the road the chronological sequence begins with an earlier house, number 20, Clarendon House (1853/57), with its own brand of fancy expressed in the large oriel over the entrance porch and the heavy, emphatic stonework with classical suggestions. This house was built for the surgeon,

THE CHARLES THACKRAH BUILDING IN THE WESTERN CAMPUS

William Braithwaite, who moved here from Park Square; his widow was still living in it at the end of the century and the medical tradition is continued in its present use as a set of consulting rooms, the entrance armoured with brass plates. Virtually contemporary is number 29, on the opposite side of the road, built for Richard Robinson of Park Row, linen manufacturer, a house with square stone quoins and heavy stone door surrounds, as if to outweigh the red brick. The next houses to be built (1857) were set alongside number 29 but were the first to essay semi-detachment: numbers 25 and 27 are solid, plain houses built for William Pepper, carting agent for the North Eastern Railway, and for George Rayner, importer of dyestuffs.

In 1859 numbers 22 and 24 were built as one house, Albert Villas, by the architect Isaiah Dixon. The first occupant of number 22, the southernmost half, was a gentleman of independent means, but industry was represented in the other half by James Bedford who had come to live above the vapours ('ammonia,

FAIRBURN HOUSE (1840) — QUEEN VICTORIA SLEPT HERE!

cudbear and orchil') of his chemical works in Kirkstall Road. The triple-columned portico half conceals the fact that these are two houses. The house was built on a sloping site levelled up, as can be seen from the surviving area basement and tradesmen's entrance down to the extensive kitchens, servants' parlour and cold stores.

It has to be said that Beresford's 'compromise' solution as to the order in which the houses on Clarendon Road are visited is not easy to follow on the ground. So we shall abandon chronology completely and begin the walk at the junction of Clarendon Road and Moorland Road, close by St Wilfrid's chapel of the former Grammar School.

Since the Grammar School moved to the outskirts of the city at Alwoodley, the site has become the Western Campus of the University. The school buildings and chapel (by E. M. Barry, son of Sir Charles Barry and brother of the then headmaster) were sympathetically converted by Carey Jones Architects in 1995. The school buildings now house the University Business School and the chapel houses the University of Leeds International Textile Archive (ULITA) and museum. Opposite, across a courtyard, and facing Clarendon Road, is the utilitarian Innovation Centre, also by Carey Jones. A deviation into the Western Campus is here called for, not only to admire (or otherwise) the curious form of the Charles Thackrah Building (again by Carey Jones) but also the Michael Marks (Marks and Spencer Archive) Building and the new Law School Building (architects: Broadway Malyan).

Returning to Clarendon Road we see on our left the rear elevations of Lyddon Terrace. From here, and until we reach Fairburn House (see below) Clarendon Road follows the line of Kendal Lane. After crossing Woodsley Road we pass, on our right, the terrace of six houses (numbers

93-83) with their long front gardens. Then, after passing Kelso Road, we see Raven House, formerly the home of the Vicar of Leeds, the setting of which is disfigured by a tall wooden fence erected in the garden. Surely Planning Permission should have been refused for such an intrusion? Further down, again on our right, Mountfields has been replaced by a block of flats of the same name.

Now we reach the cul-de-sac on the north side of Fairburn House called 'Fairburn Road' by Beresford and which marks the point where Clarendon Road deviates from Kendal Lane. Descending a short distance to the lower boundary wall we have clear views across the valley to Belle Vue Road and the abandoned buildings and playground of the former St Michael's College. To our left, hardly discernable, lies the former route of Kendal Lane, skirting the rear residential blocks of Fairburn House. Straight ahead lies the projected extension of 'Fairburn Road' to Belle Vue Road and on our right, half hidden by bushes, is a gatepost which is all that remains of Berkeley House; now (like its neighbour Mountfields) replaced by flats.

Fairburn House (now the National Institute for Health Research) was designed by John Clark in 1840-41 in a severe neo-classical style and, apart from the twentieth century residential extensions, has a chapel on the south side of 1896, designed by Temple Moore (architect of the Hostel of the Resurrection, Walk XI). It is a curious feature of Victorian planning that Fairburn House, and all the houses on the same side of Clarendon Road, were designed with their principal elevations facing the road and not overlooking the broad valley which lies to their rear.

Immediately past Fairburn House is Sheafield (No. 67), formerly the Junior School of Leeds Grammar School, the cliff-like side elevation of which faces Victoria Street, laid out by Sir Peter Fairburn as a deviation from Kendal Lane: a boundary stone, with his initials PF, is seen at the

32 AND 34 CLARENDON ROAD – SEMI-DETACHED HOUSES RESTORED
TO THEIR FORMER GLORY.

southern corner. Descending Victoria Street as far as St John's Road we see, through the iron gates on our right, the closed-off route of Kendal Lane climbing up behind Fairburn House. To our left, Kendal Lane winds its way past the north end of Hanover Square and thence back to rejoin Clarendon Road. Also on the left is Airedale Mount, overlooking the valley and now (2012) in a disgraceful state of dereliction.

Retracing our steps we can appreciate the broad sweep of Clarendon Road. It is difficult to realise that all the (even numbered) houses on the eastern side (and of course all those in Hyde Terrace) were earmarked for demolition under the Chamberlin Plan of 1960 to be replaced by hospital buildings and blocks of 'study bedrooms'. For years, they suffered from 'planning blight', a situation still very much in evidence. But since Beresford wrote there has been a very welcome 'turnaround' and the restoration of buildings (particularly numbers 22 and 24) is of a high standard. Hence Clarendon Road is resuming its former dignity as a desirable residential area and moreover one which is so close to the city centre. Even the new blocks of flats (e.g. West Mount), although lacking the flamboyance of their Victorian predecessors, maintain the scale and building line of the road.

Descending to Woodhouse Square we note, on the right, Ripon House (number 63), formerly the home of Lord Moynihan and on the left, the two short streets which lead to Hyde Terrace. The first (which has no street sign) Beresford calls 'Arthur Street', but which is called 'Hyde Place' on the present street map. Then, after number 20 Clarendon Road (with its large oriel window over the entrance porch) is Hyde Street, bordered in its south side by the northern boundary wall of Little Woodhouse Hall (Walk XIV).

Woodhouse Square is a square only in name: any sense of enclosure that may have been intended in 1825 was destroyed by the development of Clarendon Road in 1839 along its east side which originally continued over the bridge across the present Inner Ring Road to Great George Street but which now sweeps round its south side to join up with Park Lane. However, the well maintained

NUMBER 29 CLARENDON ROAD.

ALBERT VILLAS, NUMBERS 22 TO 24 CLARENDON ROAD.

and fenced-in garden make it an attractive place in which to linger and to survey the buildings around, the most prominent of which is Waverley House of 1840, by John Clark at the south-west corner. It consists, like its 'twin' at No. 30 and 32 Hyde Terrace, of two houses with just one entrance on the south front. The vacant site above Waverley House remained as such until 1904 when St Anne's R.C. School and playground were built. The school closed in 1992, the buildings were then used by Park Lane College as an annexe and were eventually demolished in 2006. On the south side the houses Nos. 2-9, now occupied by Swarthmore (Nos. 2-7) and offices (Nos. 8-9), are of 1845-46, designed by R. W. Moore, a pupil of R. D. Chantrell. No.1 (the earliest house of 1825) was demolished in 1904. These houses have seen many distinguished occupants: for example the architect, Richard Moore, (No. 3), Revd Frederick John Wood, later vicar of Headingley, (No. 4), the surgeon, Berkeley (Lord) Moynihan, (No. 5), Ellen Heaton, patron of the Arts and a supporter of women's suffrage, (No. 6), Mary Pearce, second lady Lord Mayor of Leeds, (No. 7). Then, on the east side are the much later, and much more flamboyant houses (No. 12, 1868 and No. 14, 1869) by George Corson. Within the square the sunken circular garden occupies the site of a water tank, constructed as a war time emergency measure in 1941. And overlooking all is the statue of Sir Peter Fairburn, sculpted by Matthew Noble in 1868.

STATUE OF SIR PETER FAIRBAIRN IN WOODHOUSE SQUARE.

Between number 20 Clarendon Road and Little Woodhouse Hall the short length of Hyde Street now leads only to the Dental Hospital, but being pedestrians we can use this route and pass through the traffic bollards on the left into Hyde Terrace. Had we been motorised it would have been necessary to seek the other end of the Terrace at the top of Clarendon Road.

THE BOW-SHAPE given to Clarendon Road when it was laid out by the Atkinsons had two justifications: it gave a longer frontage line for the building plots than a straight line across the fields, and it helped to reduce the gradient for carriages and carts. However, a considerable area of ground remained behind the plots in the eastern arc of the bow and a second street could be fitted in here. Although named 'terrace' it was from the beginning designed, like Springfield Terrace, as a street with houses on both sides. Since the major road had been named after the earls of Clarendon it was logical to give their family name, Hyde, to the minor development. Hyde Terrace originally joined the carriage drive from Springfield House to Leeds on the eastern side of Little Woodhouse Hall, following the high wall of the Atkinsons' garden, but this part has been obliterated and numbers 2 to 18 demolished to make room for Clarendon Way, the approach road to the Worsley Medical and Dental Building.

On the large-scale Ordnance Survey plan of 1850 the first two houses of Hyde Terrace were shown in splendid isolation as they had been since their erection a decade earlier. The made-up surface of the road petered out just beyond them and although it was eventually continued through to Clarendon Road those who pass to and from the Faversham Hotel yard along the side of numbers 30 and 32 will notice that the back lane to their coach-houses was never extended beyond the line reached in 1840 and now serves as a convenient hiding place for large dustbins.

When built in 1840, number 30 was first occupied by Frederick Baines, brother of Edward Jr, and partner in the local printing house which from 149 Briggate published the *Leeds Mercury*, the leading Liberal newspaper of provincial England, then in the van of the movement to denounce the corn laws and the landed interest. His neighbour at number 32, Edward Smith, also had premises in Briggate where he carried on a business as a woollen draper, tailor, and undertaker.

The two houses were built under one roof with a stone pediment like the houses of Georgian Leeds, but employing much plain stonework, including square-arched doors. They have matching iron balustrades for the entrance steps, and there was a wrought-iron balcony along the first floor level, now only skeletal. The architect was John Clark, who built a not dissimilar pair of houses under one roof at the south-west corner of Woodhouse Square (Waverley House) at the further end of the Atkinson development in the same year.

The protracted development, lasting from 1840 to 1891, before this short street was completed can be followed by placing the remaining buildings in chronological order. The plots next on the north of numbers 30 and 32 were unsold for another seventeen years, and although a group from 36 to 40 were built in 1857, the neighbouring number 34 was not erected until 1861 when the proprietor of the Albert Nail Works, Hunslet, William Bolland, moved from Park Square up the hill to the more salubrious Little Woodhouse just too late to be caught by the census enumerator in his new house. Moves from the old west end around Park Square were not uncommon: Frederick Baines had previously lived at 4 York Place.

Number 36, Highfield Villa, was occupied by Benjamin Russell, valuer, in 1857, the same year that two vicarages were built as numbers 38 and 40. The former was the vicarage for Holy Trinity in Boar Lane and the latter for St George's Church. The ecclesiastical atmosphere is conveyed by the cloister columns worked into the gate-posts of number 38. Number 42, the plot for which was sold in 1852, was built upon in 1856/57 by W. J. Cooper, woollen merchant, and is a sharp return to the secular in its style. It has a huge Florentine tower over its entrance hall, complete with arrow slits.

Building on the west side of the street then began with the matching trio numbers 27 to 31, a mini-terrace. Number 31 was built first, in 1858 for Godfrey Wood, confectioner; then number 29 for Thomas Greenwood, partner in the machine-making firm at the Albion Foundry; and finally number 27, 'building' at the time of the 1861 census, for F. Wood, partner in a firm of painters, gilders and decorative paper hangers. Number 25, was built in 1861 for Joshua Gibson, cloth merchant, and bears its date; number 21 (there has never been a 23) for W. J. Pritchard, 'professor of music', between 1861 and 1864 and clearly a replica of numbers 27 to 31.

Back on the east side the remaining houses show the sporadic development continuing. The plot on which numbers 44 and 46 (Woodsley Villa, now Croft Hall) stand was not built on until 1870/72, although it was sold by the Atkinsons in 1851. A single stone balustrade unifies two houses, the southern-most having a manager of a glass works as its first occupant and the other Her Majesty's Inspector of Schools. The detached house to the north, number 48, is of the same

NUMBERS 27 TO 31 HYDE TERRACE: AWAITING RESTORATION IN 2012 AND A NEW
LEASE OF LIFE.

date, occupied by Benjamin Hirst of Hirst and Brooke, manufacturing druggists, Hunslet. It formed a pair with number 52 Clarendon Road, the house of the foundry-master William Nichols.

For the next development, which did not begin until the Leeds building boom of the mid-'seventies, we must move to the other end of the same side of the street where numbers 20 to 28 form a terrace, Hyde Villas, made up of eight large houses, distinguished by high and elaborate door arches in brick and equally elaborate woodwork in their attic gables.

In 1876 numbers 15 to 19 on the opposite side of the road were built as a terrace of three identical houses as the two blocked doorways show. They were Clarendon Villa (1876), possibly designed by the architect J. Tweedle, the first occupant of number 17, although the developer was James Rhodes the clothier who lived at number 15. Number 19 was built for Nathan Bake, the wholesale grocer and provision merchant. Numbers 9 to 13 also make a trio, built on a plot of land which changed hands in 1861 and again in 1877 without any development, and then between 1886 and 1890 having three mountainous houses built on it, the earliest probably being the northern-most. Number 9, viewed from the short side-road, Arthur Street, presents the south face of a brick Eiger. The first occupants were a surgeon (number 9), a solicitor (number 11) and at number 13 the Mr Murphy who was simply a gentleman.

At the corner of Arthur Street and Hyde Terrace our survey is complete, and someone has public spiritedly placed a seat at the corner of Arthur Street and Clarendon Road where readers may rest from their labours. For the pedestrian seeking the city centre Clarendon Way leads directly past the Worsley Medical and Dental Building to the Infirmary and the Town Hall, and a variety of footpaths lead back through the University buildings to the Parkinson Steps where these Walks began.

For many years many of the buildings of Hyde Terrace served as medical departments both for the Leeds General Infirmary and the University, the rest were divided up into generally ill-planned and ill-maintained rented accommodation. No. 42 was rebuilt as the Leeds Maternity Hospital. Thus the exclusive residential character of Hyde Terrace was gradually lost and, with the closure of the Maternity Hospital and the relocation of medical departments to the new Infirmary buildings, Hyde Terrace slipped further into dereliction and decay. But the tide is now turning as is evident by the extensive works of restoration of the buildings for residential and office accommodation.

It has to be said that as in the case of Clarendon Road (*Walk XV*), as a walking itinerary, Beresford is hard to follow – nor did he intend it as such, interested as he was in the chronology of the buildings and their earliest occupants. Nor is he over-awed (as we are!) by the scale and flamboyance of the later houses. The two side-by-side vicarages, Nos. 38 and 40, the latter by George Corson are absolutely stunning – and their rear elevations look out on the mellow brown-red brick of the former Hostel of the Resurrection (*Walk XI*). This brickwork contrasts strongly with that of No. 42, the only new (*c.*1990) building in Hyde Terrace which replaces the former Maternity Hospital and now forms the entrance to the Mount Dementia Nursing Hospital. It was clearly designed to emulate the scale and proportions of the adjacent vicarages but its hard red brick and gloomy grey fenestration has not, nor is it likely, to mellow with time.

Of the other houses we may note that Nos. 30 and 32 (by John Clark) have their counterpart in Waverley House in Woodhouse Square and that the 'trio' of houses opposite, Nos. 9-13 were built by Dr Heaton and became a nursing home for Lord Moynihan, the eminent Leeds surgeon. Then, we should note the curious juxtaposition of No. 48 Hyde Terrace and No. 52 Clarendon Road: two substantial houses built 'side to back', an arrangement unconceivable today. Finally, there yet remain fragments of unidentified field and estate stone boundary walls which clearly predate the development of Hyde Terrace itself.

Regrettably, Beresford's 'seat' has long gone; nor does Arthur Street (Hyde Place) have a street sign identifying it as such (see *Walk XV*). But the 'LeedsCityBus' bus stop is not far away!

IN GENERAL THE approach to these Walks has been fully frontal, commenting on the façades of houses and paying little attention to the social significance of the back parts. Even from the front a sunken or half-sunken working basement is indicated by fanlights, steps and protective railings just as gables speak of attics that might be servant bedrooms. The census and press advertisements have been used to document some of these aspects of life below stairs and backstairs. Doubtless some have still preserved relics of bells and bell-pushes to summon servants to the drawing room or bedroom. Above stairs, although the pace of these Walks has been too rapid to give appropriate attention, it is certain that even a building converted for laboratory use can retain internal architectural details (doors, cornices, stair rails, windows, water-closets) from the first days of the house.

The absence of a front garden, particularly in the type of house that survives in the area studied, did not necessarily indicate a low social status although garden-less houses can be seen in the back-to-backs of Claremont Grove. Yet the two very large houses built in Lyddon Terrace in 1821 (numbers 11 and 13) were virtually on the pavement, as were the early houses in Woodhouse and Hanover Squares, all following the Bath and London terrace fashion. Even half a century later the large houses in Cromer Terrace and Clarendon Place were built with only token gardens. The gardens of Clarendon Road and Hyde Terrace were larger because the road was originally designed in plots for separate villas which expected to have a front carriage drive with lawn and shrubbery, although even the grandiose Woodsley House did not demand much privacy at the front.

At the rear an extensive garden did not seem to be a requirement to establish status. One definite clue to status does lie at the rear or side, however: the presence or absence of a house for coach or carriage, a stable for the horse, a hay-loft and occasionally a living-room for the groom or stableman. Mews on the scale of London or Bath did not appear in Leeds, but there were several house-less streets of convenience laid out on the assumption that access would be required by vehicles to the back of any houses to be built. One of these, on the east side of Springfield Mount, also served Mount Preston but is now elevated in status as the approach road to the Senior Common Room and the Springfield House car park.

In conclusion, the author (who himself has not been guiltless of innocent trespass in the pursuit of knowledge) must remind his readers whether they approach a building from front or rear – and particularly if entry is required – that even publicly-owned property is not for public access at all hours; some of the property within the area of the *Walks* is still privately owned, and the security of equipment and personal belongings within buildings occupied by University departments would not survive conditions of libertarian access. Certainly no arrangements have been made for a copy of these *Walks* to be acceptable as a universal passport to all the red brick of the campus. One Sunday afternoon in September 1977 a post-doctoral research fellow threatened to send for the police on seeing the author in his shrubbery – 'You're no professor, you're a thief' was the reaction to a hurried explanation. I do not blame his diagnosis: he could well have been right.

THE ORDNANCE SURVEY did not reach this part of Leeds until 1847 and the work of those years was embodied in the sheets of the finely-drawn maps on a scale of sixty inches to the mile, large enough for drives, shrubberies, greenhouses, outhouses, and stables to be drawn. The first map on the six-inch (1851) and one-inch (1858) scales used the same material.

Before 1847 the development of property in Woodhouse must be followed on privately published maps and on manuscript surveys made for individual owners and developers. The intervals between the published maps are too large for precise dating of individual buildings; and it was not unknown for cartographers, who were local surveyors, to anticipate a development that some economic stringency had in fact caused to be postponed. Directories likewise did not achieve regular and frequent revision until the late nineteenth century, and in them larger houses were often described simply as 'Little Woodhouse'; the better villas often (as today) flattered their social status by preferring a house-name to a number and – even more confusingly – changed their name from time to time. Number 19 Springfield Mount, now used as flats by medical staff from the Maternity Hospital, was Bethel House in 1842, Springfield Crescent [sic] in 1853 and Mount Villas in 1876 after the house had been divided. Division of houses, even the largest, was not unknown. We have already seen that Denison Hall was divided as soon as its builder, John Wilkinson Denison, left for Nottinghamshire, and the present Faversham Hotel began its life as one house (c.1844) but by 1853 was divided into two as Springfield Villas, later Spring Lea.

Under clause 166 of the Leeds Improvement Act of 1842 it was compulsory for houseowners to allow their front gates, however grand, to have black-and-white painted numbers to assist identification for rating purposes. The census enumerators of 1851, whose detailed human inventories survive for consultation, were often content to omit house numbers. Were it not for surviving property deeds (with the Bursary, the Hospital solicitors, the City Archives, the West Yorkshire County Record Office, and in private hands) it would be quite impossible to use for house-dating the six names that the census of 1841 assigned to 'Springfield Mount' but without house-names or numbers and not in any geographical order: indeed two of the six families were almost certainly in Mount Preston, indicating the difficulty that a census enumerator had with fields where 'intended streets' had only a few scattered building plots yet taken up.

The property deeds and the printed Statements of Title that were usually issued by the developers' solicitors give the clearest indication available of the land sales preceding building, the mortgages associated with building or later embarrassments, and the names and occupations of the persons concerned, as well as the sums that changed hands. Only a minority of deeds at that period included a plan although would-be developers sometimes issued estate plans: the earliest evidence for number 27 Springfield Mount, now incorporated in the Mount Medical Residences, is one such plan printed in January 1839 at an early state in the Atkinsons' efforts to populate the Clarendon Road venture.

The deeds for a larger house may sometimes describe its appearance although usually 'capital messuage' would suffice. Recent work in the unindexed and voluminous records of the Sun and Royal Exchange fire insurance companies has enabled both dating and description of buildings to be amplified, but for description there is nothing to better the sales talk of the advertisements when the larger Georgian houses were being offered for sale or rent in the columns of the Leeds newspapers, the *Mercury* and the *Intelligencer*.

The house-by-house census enumerator's books are available at the Public Record Office, London for 1841, 1851, 1861, and 1871. The Leeds City Reference Library has microfilms available for study, together with street-indexes. The same Library has the most complete collection of local directories. There is an incomplete set of town rate books in the City Archives Department but even this series has not been preserved beyond 1805. The same Department has a large collection of documents from the offices of solicitors whose clients were involved in the development of this red brick area of Leeds.

Much of the building development which Beresford records in *Walks Round Red Brick* is covered in Chapter 10 in his *magnus opus* on Leeds: *East End, West End; the Face of Leeds during Urbanisation 1684-1842*, published by the Thoresby Society in 1988. Here he points out (p. 328), with respect to the earliest buildings, that 'What even these surviving buildings cannot show, however, is the full range of original outbuildings, for only fragments survive ... Thus they misleadingly appear to be solely residences whereas all, from Denison Hall down to the smallest, were designed to combine home and finishing shops in the continuing tradition of Leeds merchants before they aspired to be gentlemen'.

Beresford also summarises (p. 321) the progress of demolition:

'Up to 1945 no villas had been demolished except Mount Pleasant taken for the site of the Leeds General Infirmary ... and Beech Grove, demolished in 1884 when the Yorkshire College's Dyeing Department was built. After 1945 the topography of the former villa territory was radically changed, producing not only the demolition of many villas ... but the massive demolition of streets, rows and terraces ... which enabled the area to be partitioned like some latter-day Poland for the benefit of the two campuses of the University and the Polytechnic'.

He also mentions his own participation at a midnight wake (7 March 1978) on the eve of an eviction order at Belmont 'with the contractor's bulldozers pawing the ground outside'.

Beresford also contributed a substantial article on the building development of the University entitled 'Red Brick and Portland Stone, a Building History in Studies', in *The History of a University 1874-1974* edited by P. H. J. H. Gosden and A. J. Taylor, (Leeds, 1975) and published to commemorate the centenary of the University (from the founding of the Yorkshire College). It is greatly to be regretted that the volume proposed to commemorate the centenary in 2004 of the founding of the University itself never saw the light of day.

Since then the University campus has been covered in Susan Wrathmell's *Leeds* volume of the Pevsner Architectural Guides (2005) and most recently in 'The Buildings of England' volume *Yorkshire West Riding: Leeds Bradford and the North* by Peter Leach and Nikolaus Pevsner (2009). These two books have been invaluable in establishing building dates and architects of buildings, both those described by Beresford and those which are only included in the present revision. Wrathmell's and Leach's descriptions are so precise that it has been difficult to avoid paraphrasing them. Elain Harwood's monograph *Chamberlin, Powell and Bon* in the RIBA series on 20th Century Architects (RIBA Publishing, 2011) covers their University buildings in detail. Earlier University buildings are covered in *Building a Great Victorian City: Leeds Architects and Architecture 1790-1914*, edited by Christopher Webster (Huddersfield, Northern Heritage Publications, 2011).